Hedge Witchcraft and Druidry

A Guide to Divination, Spellcraft, Celtic Paganism, Druidism, Animism, Folk Magic, and Rituals of Solitary Druids

© Copyright 2023 - All rights reserved.

The content contained within this book may not be reproduced, duplicated, or transmitted without direct written permission from the author or the publisher.

Under no circumstances will any blame or legal responsibility be held against the publisher, or author, for any damages, reparation, or monetary loss due to the information contained within this book, either directly or indirectly.

Legal Notice:

This book is copyright protected. It is only for personal use. You cannot amend, distribute, sell, use, quote, or paraphrase any part, or the content within this book, without the consent of the author or publisher.

Disclaimer Notice:

Please note the information contained within this document is for educational and entertainment purposes only. All effort has been executed to present accurate, up-to-date, reliable, and complete information. No warranties of any kind are declared or implied. Readers acknowledge that the author is not engaging in the rendering of legal, financial, medical, or professional advice. The content within this book has been derived from various sources. Please consult a licensed professional before attempting any techniques outlined in this book.

By reading this document, the reader agrees that under no circumstances is the author responsible for any losses, direct or indirect, that are incurred as a result of the use of the information contained within this document, including, but not limited to, errors, omissions, or inaccuracies.

Your Free Gift
(only available for a limited time)

Thanks for getting this book! If you want to learn more about various spirituality topics, then join Mari Silva's community and get a free guided meditation MP3 for awakening your third eye. This guided meditation mp3 is designed to open and strengthen ones third eye so you can experience a higher state of consciousness. Simply visit the link below the image to get started.

https://spiritualityspot.com/meditation

Table of Contents

PART 1: HEDGE WITCHCRAFT 1
   INTRODUCTION 2
   CHAPTER 1: WHAT IS HEDGE WITCHCRAFT? 4
   CHAPTER 2: THE HEDGE MIND AND OTHER TOOLS OF
   THE CRAFT 12
   CHAPTER 3: DEITIES YOU CAN WORK WITH 18
   CHAPTER 4: HEDGE RIDING AND THE OTHER WORLD 26
   CHAPTER 5: SPIRIT ALLIES AND HOW TO FIND THEM 34
   CHAPTER 6: MAGICAL HERBS, PLANTS, AND TREES 45
   CHAPTER 7: HEDGE DIVINATION 52
   CHAPTER 8: KITCHEN MAGIC 61
   CHAPTER 9: SACRED SABBATS AND RITUALS 69
   CHAPTER 10: YOUR HEDGE SPELL BOOK 78
   CONCLUSION 89
PART 2: HEDGE DRUIDRY 91
   INTRODUCTION 92
   CHAPTER 1: FROM DRUIDRY TO HEDGE DRUIDRY 94
   CHAPTER 2: THE AWEN AND CELTIC COSMOLOGY 103
   CHAPTER 3: OPENING YOUR MIND TO NATURE 112
   CHAPTER 4: MEET YOUR SPIRIT ALLIES 120
   CHAPTER 5: MOVING TO THE OTHERWORLD 130
   CHAPTER 6: SACRED HERBS, PLANTS, AND TREES 139
   CHAPTER 7: READING THE TREE ALPHABET 143

CHAPTER 8: OGHAM DIVINATION 153
CHAPTER 9: SACRED DAYS AND HOW TO CELEBRATE
THEM ALONE... 159
CHAPTER 10: SPELLS AND RITUALS 169
CONCLUSION... 177
HERE'S ANOTHER BOOK BY MARI SILVA THAT YOU MIGHT LIKE 179
YOUR FREE GIFT (ONLY AVAILABLE FOR A LIMITED TIME).................. 180
REFERENCES 181

Part 1: Hedge Witchcraft

A Solitary Witch's Guide to Divination, Spellcraft, Celtic Paganism, Rituals, and Folk Magic

Introduction

Have you ever wondered what it would be like to perform hedge witchcraft? From traditional folklore, hedge witches use quick, easy-to-find ingredients found in most people's kitchens to create and cast spells for various purposes. Hedge witches, also known as cunning folk, have been around for centuries and perform their magical practices without anyone to supervise or teach them. Often called "the knowledge of the wise woman," hedge-witchcraft is based on folklore and encompasses magic traditions.

Hedge witchcraft can be used by anyone who has an interest in magic, whether they are a beginner or more experienced. Anyone who wants to increase their magical ability will find many uses for this powerful form of magic. However, this book is not open to anyone who desires to use hedge witchcraft dangerously or hurt others. You must be sure that you only use the craft for good, which means following written instructions and setting positive intentions. Why? Because anyone can use hedge-witchcraft tools to harm another person if they do not follow the rules and understand exactly what they are doing.

Traditional hedge witchcraft uses charms, incantations, and herbal remedies to accomplish goals. However, there are no specific rules of practice regarding hedge witchcraft. Many traditionalists practice alone or with a group of fellow practitioners. The purpose of this book is to provide a solid foundation for those looking for further personal development by practicing traditional hedge witchcraft. If you are already a practitioner, you'll get even more information about the craft from this book. Nothing in this book is intimidating or difficult to learn. You'll get all the tools you need to get started, including lists of required basic materials. With these lists and by following the simple directions, anyone can practice hedge witchcraft.

The mysticism behind the practice of hedge witchcraft is simple but effective. The use of common household herbs, such as sage and thyme, evokes the mystical effects of magic once commonly practiced in Europe. Although these methods seem quite primitive in today's world, many people are still practicing under these guidelines. Unlike other books on this topic, this one is written in simple English, making it easy to understand. The instructions are straightforward, in a step-by-step approach that takes you by the hand and walks you through what you need to do to achieve your goals with hedge witchcraft. The result is that you can practice what you learn in this book with the confidence of a seasoned hand. You will learn about the roots of the practice of hedge witchcraft, the concepts behind it, spells, and charms for different purposes, such as love, protection, healing, etc. Not only will you find out what ingredients you need to perform each spell or ritual here, but you'll also know what each one is for. If you're ready to begin your journey as a hedge witch, let's get into it.

Chapter 1: What Is Hedge Witchcraft?

Practicing hedge witchcraft is like channeling information from nature, from the Earth itself. The practitioner of hedge witchcraft can attune themselves to natural cycles and energies we don't encounter in everyday society. The practitioner of hedge witchcraft becomes a part of their environment more subtly, giving their perception an empathic boost and the ability to be more connected with their surroundings.

The craft comprises aspects of green magic, kitchen magic, and folk magic, along with spirit work, animism, and Celtic paganism. So, without further ado, let's get into these topics, so you can gain a better understanding of what hedge witchcraft is.

Green Magic

As its name suggests, this magic works with plants, crystals, gems, and their energies. You can use them as a form of therapy for the spirit or magical intentions. The green witch always works with herbs and is very in touch with nature. The idea is that there is power in the color green since it is one of the most abundant colors of Mother Nature. It's useful for healing and abundance.

Green witches work with herbs.
https://unsplash.com/photos/kcvRHtAyuig?utm_source=unsplash&utm_medium=referral&utm_content=creditShareLink

The green witch will follow a set of values aligned with nature and the Earth. Those who practice this form of magic are usually closely in touch with their energetic life force and celebrate regular rituals and rites. They work with divination, herbalism, and healing, believing that plants have specific energy, just as crystals do. For example, the moon, sun, and planets are all-powerful energy sources. Anyone who practices green magic believes that all these energies are active and that the more you can connect with them, the better you will feel.

Green witches believe in the power of flowers. They take the wonder of blooming flowers very seriously and work with them regularly to help them to find balance and peace. The green witch will often use the power of flowers during healing and also use them during magical ceremonies.

Green magic focuses on nature, the Earth, and all it offers. Followers believe in working with Mother Nature, celebrating her, helping her when she needs help, and working alongside her to achieve balance.

Kitchen Magic

Kitchen magic involves everything about the kitchen and cooking. It's a fusion of cuisine and witchcraft. The entire practice revolves around food and how you can combine different ingredients to produce magical effects. Every spice and herb used in cooking has a very real effect on our energies, and the kitchen witch knows how to combine and amplify them to help those who eat from her table.

To feel the power of kitchen magic, you must include all the things that please you and make you happy in your cooking. You should include complementary ingredients to what you cook, so they bring out the best in the meal. It's funny how some people don't value their kitchen as much as they should, let alone the process of feeding themselves or others. Making a meal from scratch with your own hands can be very magical, and it makes it even better to enjoy the works of your hands or enjoy the fact that everyone else is being fed thanks to your work, physically and spiritually. In other words, kitchen magic is a craft that encourages mindfulness, and mindfulness is a state that allows the power of magic to be even more pronounced.

The goal of this practice is to be able to create harmony in your own home. You should be able to connect with people who eat at your table and make them feel at home. To practice this form of magic, you need to be at home with your kitchen and the ingredients you've got, making sure you're always stocked for whatever magical needs you may have.

It is helpful to have an altar in the kitchen for this practice. You could consider the kitchen stove the same as the historical hearth, where every kitchen witch would prep her food. You want a portable altar; on it, you can put your candle, cauldron, a statue of your goddess, or whatever you want. It's also essential that the kitchen space be kept clean, not just physically but spiritually. It's easy to assume that all you need to do is wipe things down, and that's the end of that. In reality, you need to use sage to keep the place spiritually clean.

Suppose you're going to practice as a kitchen witch. In that case, it can be as simple as infusing every meal prep moment with magical intentions. For instance, you could intend that every ingredient you touch will generate love, healing, or abundance for those who enjoy the meal. You can also bring the other people around you in on the magic by having them mindfully set intentions for the meal you've prepared before everyone digs in to eat. Every spoonful of food could be used as a magical ritual to help you manifest your desires.

Folk Magic

This is the kind of magic of the common folk, and it's nothing like the ceremonial magic associated with those you think of as "elite." This is a very practical form of magic, and its intention is to deal with simple things like bringing more love and luck into your life, healing you, keeping bad energies away from you and your loved ones, helping you attain abundance, fertility, or finding what you've lost, as well as being able to recognize omens. The rituals performed in this kind of magic are simple and involve materials like wood, plants, twine, feathers, nails, animals, iron, eggshells, cowries, and so on.

It is important to note that folk magic is the type practiced by specific cultures and traditions. They will have specific rules for how you should interact with the world. Folk magic has many elements other kinds of magic borrow from, and, as a result, it can be confusing trying to differentiate it from other forms of magic. However, it all stems from the same ancient practices, which can be adapted to what you need them to be. Folk magic isn't connected to one specific religion, and there isn't a pantheon of specific gods that need to be worshiped. You don't need to adhere to a specific body of beliefs either. So, you could be a Buddhist or an Atheist and practice this form of magic and get phenomenal results.

Folk magic is all about sacred tradition. The term "sacred tradition" is one of the most common names given to traditional beliefs, customs, and practices that are important to people in a society. They're passed down from generation to generation, and people often look to them for guidance, wisdom, and comfort when such things are needed. This kind of magic looks at the world around us in tiny details and makes a safety net out of them. You'll see small symbolic gestures have a huge impact on your life.

Spirit Work

It's a little hard to explain, but Spirit Work is a name we've given the practice of connecting with the spiritual energies around us. We work with specific aspects of these energies and entities. While that seems pretty abstract, it has real-world effects on people daily.

The idea is that you are connecting with the spiritual energies in your life. Everyone experiences these energies to one degree or another, but not everyone is focused on them. Spiritual energy is a part of everything and flows all around us. You know when you are in a good place, and you feel great? That's because there is spiritual energy all around you that is in alignment, causing things to go right. Spirit work lets you take advantage of this energy instead of waiting and hoping that things begin to go your way. You can harness the energy and channel it to whatever real-world results you want to accomplish.

Spirit work involves being in touch with spirits to perform magic. It means working with spiritual practitioners like witches and shamans, as they can traverse the realms between worlds that we cannot detect with our physical eyes. Wiccans also do spirit work by casting magic circles to contact spirits to enlist their help. As for witches, they don't need magic circles. Mediums are the ones who make spirit work available to the masses, helping regular people to contact the spirits of their loved ones who have passed on or other beings that do not exist in our world. This form of magic is something that came to be more popular as Spiritualism became more mainstream between 1840 and 1930.

Spirit work is also known as necromancy, which means conjuring the spirits of those who have passed on to learn about the future or how to change things for the better. These spirits can lend us their energies and knowledge to help the magical practitioner to perform their spells and rituals and get actual results from their work. For some practitioners, it's about ordering the spirits to do what they want. For others, it's about developing a relationship with these entities and respectfully enlisting their help in return for offerings.

Animism

The idea behind animism is that everything has its spirit. Whether you consider the thing to be living or nonliving doesn't matter. Everything has an essence with which you can interact. Animism is integral when it comes to spirituality. Every thing and every place has its own spirit, which is connected to the spirit of every other thing and people around them. It forms the core of various beliefs, practices, and forms of magic. Animism goes as far back as the Paleolithic era.

The word "animism" is from the Latin word anima, which means "life, spirit, or breath." it's the animating power that lies in all things and all beings. When it comes to animism, the idea is that you can draw on the spirits of the rocks, mountains, rivers, art, animals, plants, and more to perform your magical work. The idea of everything possessing a spirit is a very common one outside the Western world that they don't have a specific word that connotes the idea. It is taken for granted that all things are animated and that the life force within can be activated to do one's bidding.

Animism goes so far as to make clear that words and ideas are also imbued with their life force. Therefore, this school of thought holds that things like your name or the name of your hometown could have a very real effect on your life, for better or worse.

Celtic Paganism

The Celtic people of the Iron Age created their unique form of spirituality that mixed pagan and Christian elements. They were the first "pagans" to convert to Christianity due to the influence of missionaries from Iona in Scotland, but many of their stories and traditions had already disappeared.

Celtic paganism is polytheistic, meaning they worship and make sacrifices to more than one god. Many lesser gods may be connected to the more important gods. The Celtic people used many of the same religious symbols as people in other parts of the world did, but each group had its own variations.

Celtic is an adjective, not a noun, describing a group of people that lived in Europe before and during classical times. They spoke Celtic languages and worshiped similar deities to those found in other areas with Celtic populations.

The Celts were spread out over a wide geographic area, and religious traditions varied greatly. However, there were some commonalities. Celtic religious practices included offerings to nature spirits and ancestors when asking for help to cure illness and provide prosperity. They used divination to learn the truth when needed and held festivals dedicated to the various gods.

What Is Hedge Witchcraft?

Hedge witchcraft is one of the more popular pagan paths. There are so many ideas about what it means to be a hedge witch, but the main characteristic of it is that it requires a lot of herbs and a strong connection with nature. You could also do magical work with your preferred goddesses and gods as a hedge witch. You can also act as a shaman and a healer or even affect the weather. That's the thing about being a hedge witch. It's a blend of all the other forms of crafts that we've covered.

Let's dig into the history of this form of witchcraft a bit because, for the most part, practitioners do just that to honor the past. Historically, witches were usually women and didn't live in the community of villagers. Instead, they lived on the fringes, usually on the hedgerows' other side. The hedge was a significant divider because, on one side, you would see the typical village life or civilization as it was back then, but on the other side, it was completely different. On the other side of the hedge lived the unknown, all the things the villagers considered wild.

The hedge witches acted as healers, helping those who needed help with some illness or injury. They were also rather cunning in their ways. As part of their job, they also took their time collecting essential plants and herbs from the deep forests and the hedges.

Hedge witchcraft was a solo craft that back then would be practiced alone. It was also not separate from daily life, in that even little acts like cleaning your home or making a nice pot of tea were considered a magical process, as you can imbue it with intentions for what you want to manifest. The hedge witch back then would learn her craft from other people in the family who had been practicing for a while and had honed their craft through practice. Sometimes you'll hear hedge witchcraft being called the green craft. At all times, you can expect to see a lot of influence from folk magic.

Like kitchen witchcraft, hedge witchcraft primarily revolves around the hearth and home, just as kitchen magic does. Your home is where you come from, representing your sense of stability. In your home, you feel grounded. Your home has a unique energy, affecting family and visitors who leave their own energetic imprint.

As hedge witchcraft revolves around the hearth and home, it is strongly rooted in the natural world. This means you must do a fair bit of herbal magic, including aromatherapy work. Often, hedge witchcraft involves using plants and herbs you've grown with your own hands. You'll likely have processed them on your own, drying what you need to and storing them in a way that works for you. You'll have looked into all your herbs, understood their energies, and learned how you could blend them all to make them work for you. The whole time, a true hedge witch also takes notes in a special grimoire so they can refer to the information later and not mix things up.

Advantages of Practicing Hedge Witchcraft

An advantage of practicing hedge witchcraft is that it doesn't require any formal training or initiation. A person can put on their first witch's hat and start practicing hedge witchcraft immediately if they want. People also say that being self-taught helps them identify with their abilities more than being taught by someone else, making them feel more comfortable experimenting with what they learn.

Another advantage of practicing hedge witchcraft is that it allows the practitioner to learn about witchcraft without having to shock their friends and family by telling them about their beliefs. It also allows them to learn about the craft without joining a coven or attending witchcraft classes.

Some say there are also disadvantages to practicing hedge witchcraft, particularly when you're going solo. They say they have mixed feelings about some of the practices they engage in because they aren't familiar with what other witches think is right or wrong and because whatever they have learned has come from books, magazines, websites, or other people's experiences. But the thing about this craft is you can't get it wrong as long as you know the basics and your intentions are clear and pure.

How can hedge witchcraft change your life for the better? It is great to help you to clear away distractions and to take control of your life. It's also good at allowing you to be more precise and precise in your abilities by learning to feel the energy around you and tweak it with your own.

Some people say that some of the best things they have accomplished in life have come after they began practicing hedge witchcraft, thanks largely to using the craft more effectively, developing better intuition about people and situations, and personal growth.

Are You a Hedge Witch?

1. Are you drawn to herbs?
2. Have you ever felt a connection to plants?
3. Do you get the sense that you can work magic with plants and herbs?
4. Do you feel a strong connection to nature?
5. Do you feel terrible if you haven't been out in nature for a while?

If you answered yes to at least three of these five questions, hedge witchcraft could be for you.

Chapter 2: The Hedge Mind and Other Tools of the Craft

The mind is the most important tool for practicing hedge witchcraft. In fact, the mind gives all other tools their power and effectiveness. As a result, mental discipline is crucial to the practice of hedge witchcraft. Mental discipline allows individuals to hone their psychic abilities, so they can more effectively connect with the natural world and receive positive outcomes in life while drawing down harmful influences from those around them.

What Is the Mind?

The mind is the consciousness of an individual. It connects to and interacts with the universe and everything in it, including other people, animals, nature, spirits, gods, goddesses, etc. With practice, individuals can enhance their connection to their minds and their minds' ability to recognize existing connections. In this way, they can develop a new understanding of themselves within the world around them and learn to control various situations and events that would otherwise be beyond their influence. To hedge witches, the mind is a powerful and useful tool that should be used to improve oneself and others.

How Can I Develop My Mind?

There are many practices an individual can perform to develop their mind. The most basic approach is to meditate or use some other type of focusing exercise where you become completely still and then focus on your thoughts, thus quieting the mind. Mindfulness and meditation are two very different concepts that can be practiced for many benefits.

The practice of mindfulness essentially allows an individual to become aware of the moment, what interactions are taking place, and also be aware of their thoughts and emotions. The practice of mindfulness helps you learn to recognize your physical and emotional states by becoming more connected to them. Practicing mindfulness could also help you control your emotions, which can be a powerful advantage when healing or restoring others.

Meditation is the practice of quieting one's thoughts and focusing on one thing, usually a crystal or candle flame. Meditation relaxes the mind and allows individuals to focus on the work that they are trying to do. Meditation can also help individuals to strengthen their psychic abilities by increasing their mental clarity. Connecting when confusing or chaotic thoughts aren't bombarding your mind is easier.

It is said that the human mind has two complementary parts. One part of the brain is used for logic and analysis, which helps you process information to make accurate decisions. The other part of the brain deals with feelings, memories, instincts, and intuition. You can use a greater portion of either or both parts by training your mind, depending on your goal. Turning your thoughts inward and connecting with the feeling part of your mind can enhance your psychic abilities and relationships with others.

Being mindful of your thoughts and emotions and connecting to feel-good emotions can help you overcome negative feelings from past experiences. This can be beneficial because past negative experiences are often based on feelings of loneliness, fear, or insecurity and can trigger the same feelings in you again. You need to be in a positive state of mind if you achieve your goals through hedge witchcraft. A positive mindset allows you to become more connected to life. In turn, this can help you become aware of opportunities often overlooked by others, which is essential when working with hedge witchcraft.

How to Get into the Right Mindset

1. **Meditate:** Just focus on your breathing and nothing else for about five to ten minutes each day. When your mind wanders (and it will), just be glad you noticed and bring your attention back to your

breath. Do this as many times as you get distracted. You'll get better at this the more you practice, and soon it will be very easy to get into a state of Zen without needing much time or effort.

2. **Spend Time in Nature:** Take time to enjoy nature daily, even if it's just for five minutes. Enjoy the aromas, the feel of the air against your skin, listen to the sounds, and look at the plants and trees (or, in my case, listen to the birds). Each day you'll find you need less time in nature. And when you spend time in nature, ensure you have a positive attitude toward what you see. When your mind is focused on appreciation and beauty, your attitude will follow suit. You should also try walking on the ground barefoot, and it will center you.

3. **Enjoy the Positive Aspects of Your Life:** Enjoy the things that make you happy. Whether it's getting to sleep in, a meditative bath, a good workout, or just reading a good book - take time to enjoy and appreciate these things. Know that they can always be there; you're lucky to have them.

4. **Take Time for Yourself:** Take at least one day each week when you do not have to worry about your job, finances, bills, or any other stress. Give yourself the freedom to spend these hours sleeping in, going for a stroll in nature, or simply enjoying a cup of coffee and reading a book.

5. **Follow Your Passions:** Pursue activities you love and feel good while doing them. Find a hobby that you can do for a lifetime. You'll find you'll enjoy it more, and doing it will bring you joy - in the same way that anything else that brings you joy does.

Tools Needed in Hedge Witchcraft

You don't need to break the bank to get these tools. When you know the purpose of each one, you can work with regular materials around your home. For instance, you could use a cooking pot dedicated to your magic instead of a cauldron. If you want to buy tools specifically crafted for the craft but don't want to spend too much, consider checking Craigslist or eBay.

The Cauldron: A large pot (often round) used to prepare and cook food. This is the main tool that you will use to start witching. It must be made from copper and have a lid that fits well on top. An old saucepan, cast-iron pan, or baking dish can also work. Every witch owns one; it's a cliché, sure. But if you find yourself in a situation where your cauldron is ruined or out of use, and you don't have the funds to buy a new one, then consider renting one from a local theatrical store.

The Wand: A long, thin stick or branch used to direct energy. In many traditions, it is made from a tree branch. The wand must be made of wood and cannot be plastic or metal. In some aspects of magic, the wand also represents a phallic symbol, so if this makes you uncomfortable, then you can use something like a dowsing rod instead. It's not always used in witchcraft, but it is useful when you need to call upon the element of air, which is one of the major elements in most traditions.

The Mortar and Pestle: Used to crush and mix ingredients together. The mortar is just a bowl, and the pestle is the stick you rub inside it to crush ingredients. You need these two together to successfully handcraft your spells. Be sure to get one that fits well in your hand and is made of wood with a long handle.

Use a mortar and pestle to crush your materials.
https://unsplash.com/photos/9-Hgi9w9bDM?utm_source=unsplash&utm_medium=referral&utm_content=creditShareLink

The Athame: This tool is like a wand, but instead of directing energy, it cuts energy. It is used for cutting up herbs and candles. The athame is usually double-edged and made of metal so that it can effectively cut what you are working with. Also called a black-handled knife or a white-handled knife, depending on the tradition you are part of. This is also used for drawing symbols or words in the air. It can also be used for carving symbols into candles or working with a candle.

The Athame Sheath: This is a cover that you will use to keep your athame safe while not using it. You can make one yourself or buy one at many places, including online stores.

The Grimoire: A book of spells and rituals. It's a book of magic. This spiritual tool you'll use to write out and record your spells. You can and should have your own, but you can find published grimoires in bookstores, or sometimes you may find one at a library. These books also come in different styles and sizes. Be sure to get one that you can use comfortably and with room for your spell-writing needs. There are many on the market, but these can be expensive. An alternative is to look online for free spells, test those spells out, and then write them in your own grimoire. It's also known as the Book of Shadows.

The Bell: Is often used to clear energy in the area you are working in. You can also use it to call upon the elements of nature. The bell should be a small one that is not too loud but enough to catch your attention when it rings. A small bell or chime can also call on spirits or mark the end of a spell's spoken words.

Crystals and Stones: These are considered "energetic tools" that act as a mirror for the energy of an object. These can be used in several ways depending on what belief system you are part of. They can be used to create spells, call spirits, and communicate with them (through your own voice or a recording). Many witches also keep stones in their bags or pockets to ground themselves. Some stones are believed to hold magical powers and are used for protection. You can get these from various sources, but you must be careful where you get them; you need to be sure they are authentic. Some of the most common crystals used in witchcraft are quartz, amethyst, jasper, and citrine.

The Bellows: This tool is used for blowing out candles and sending energy into objects such as candles, incense, and crystals. You can also use it for blowing on a person to help them relax and sleep.

The Broom: Used to cleanse negative energy from an area, it is yet another common witch cliché. You can use a "real" broom, but it is unnecessary. You can also use a feather duster or a feather if you do not have access to any other tools. The broom is also used in some spells where a need arises to "sweep" something away (pushing energy downward instead of upward). It can also be used for cleaning the floor and walls during a spell. Many witches also use brooms to clear the air in an area during rituals or spell casting.

The Knife: Used to cut or slice herbs; one of these would also be useful while cooking at home. You could use scissors instead.

Divination Tools: These are used for readings and messages from spirits. You can also use them to find out information about a spell you want to make or the magical impact it will have on you, a person, or an object. Many traditions use tarot cards in various ways and can be used in conjunction with other tools. Runes are also used in some traditions, including witchcraft.

The Tarot Deck or Card Set: If you use a tarot deck or other divination tool, you will need to have a tool to shuffle the cards. Several decks exist, and the one that you choose should reflect the type of magical beliefs that you have. Most decks also come with a few spreads, such as "readings" and "expert readings," to help you to create your own spells and rituals. These are separate from the cards and do not need to cast spells. The images on cards can also have different meanings depending on which deck you use. You also get a book to help you interpret all of these meanings, which is almost always a great idea.

The Velvet Bag: This bag can hold small objects such as herbs that you may need during a spell, and it can also be used to hold your other tools during spell casting.

Sigils: Sigils are a visual picture to represent the magic that you want to do. They can be used to cast spells, draw power from objects, and create a spiritual connection. You can create your own or buy them, and there are also kits you can use to help you create your sigil. In many traditions, these symbols are carved into candles or other objects representing energy.

Small Jars and Containers: Used for holding herbs, spices, and other items. Symbols and sigils painted or drawn on the container can also help you to cast spells and call upon spirits.

Chapter 3: Deities You Can Work With

Hedge witchcraft has a deep connection to Celtic paganism. So, we'll talk about the important deities that the Celts honor. You don't have to work with all of these deities, and it's up to you to figure out who resonates with you the most and then work with them instead. When you have an energetic or spiritual bond with a deity, you can draw on that connection to imbue your rituals with power.

Brigid

Brigid is known as "the Exalted One." She rules over motherhood and fertility. If you're a poet, an inventor, into some sort of craft, or you're a very passionate person, you have her to thank for that. Pagans believe there are three parts to this goddess, just as is the case with some other deities, but the difference is that each part is named the same.

For some, there are a lot of parallels between Brigid the goddess and the Christian Saint Brigid of Kildare. She is believed to simply be the Catholic Church's attempt to syncretize the land's spirituality with their religion. Her symbol is a cross with three arms, sometimes four. This cross is made of rushes, and it is believed that if you want to keep yourself safe and protected, all you have to do is put it over your window or door at home, and she'll protect you.

This goddess influences life and springtime, when everything thrives and comes to life. She is in charge of the smithery and the one to turn to when you work with the healing arts. She is celebrated on Imbolc, which happens each year on the first of February, being the middle of winter. If you go to Ireland, you'll find that the people have dedicated most of the waterways and wells to this deity. Brigid is part of the Tuatha Dé Danann.

Originally, her name was Brid, until it was anglicized into the current form and the other names Bride, Brig, and Brigit. The goddess's name inspired the name Bridget, demonstrating her link to fire and the sun. It's also possibly connected to other Indo-European goddesses in charge of the dawn. She wears a sunbeam cloak, demonstrating her fire and passion, but she's also in charge of water and serenity. She can show up either as a mother figure or a lovely maiden. Her hair is reminiscent of fire itself, and she rules the dawn.

Brigid knows all there is to know about high architecture and inspires people in that field and other craftsmen. She is wise and a healer, both attributes she inherited from Dagda, her father, who reigned supreme in matters of mysticism and magic. She also knows what your true needs are at every moment. There is a well dedicated to her in Kildare, and its waters are used for healing and blessing. There's also another well dedicated to her in County Clare.

Brigid was the daughter of one of the chiefs of the Tuatha Dé Danann named Dagda, and thanks to him, she had many sisters and brothers, including Midir and Aengus. Danu, the river goddess, was her mother. Brigid had a son with Bres, her husband, named Ruadan. Some other lore holds that she was married to Tuireann instead and had three sons named Irchaba, Iuchar, and Brian. Her sons were responsible for killing Lugh's father, Cian. It is known that many strangers come to Brigid to ask her to heal, bless, and inspire them. She favors those who have good intentions and those who are cunning.

Worshiping Brigid

You can honor her on February 1. This is the start of the New Year in Ireland, and on this day, you can take coins and food offerings to any waterway close by to honor her. As you make your offerings, you can also ask her to protect, heal, guide, and inspire you. You can ask her to bless your family and children, or even your pets if you've got any. You may offer her water, fire, metals, and prayer. You could get ribbons and tie them to a tree in her honor. She also likes coins, ale, cakes, poetry, and eggs. Do you have a basket constructed from rushes? Bring that to her, and you will have her heart.

Cernunnos

This is the god in charge of the wild. He ruled over the beasts of the land and is often depicted as having a horn, with animals all around him. He is adept at brokering peace between enemies. There are several other horned gods he shares a link with, as well as the Green Man, Herne the Hunter, Silvanus, and Pan. There's proof that it was mostly the people of the land of Gaul who worshiped this horned god, though. You can refer to him as the horned one.

This god has a way of bringing peace between nature and humans, and he's the one who can tame animals to the point where predator and prey can find peace with each other. Sadly, his actual myth remains a mystery. His name, though, is a Gaelic word that means "horned one," and lately, it's become the name to use when referring to the other horned gods the Celts used to worship, whose names have now been forgotten. To neopagans, he is the "God of Wild Places" or the "Lord of the Wilds," both titles being very recent developments.

A man with a beard and antlers, either wearing or carrying a torc made of metal, is believed that his physical attributes are put together based on other deities from Rome and Greece who looked similar. He was basically a merger of several gods. He would bless his followers not only with animals but with vegetables and fruit. He's often depicted with snakes, aurochs, wolves, and an elk, all residing side by side because he can easily quash enmity between natural foes. This makes him the god to seek protection and provision from.

It is believed that Cernunnos has a connection to Conach Cernach, at least etymologically speaking. Conach Cernach is from the Ulster cycle. Cernunnos may also share some links to Shakespeare's Herne the Hunter, who killed himself rather than be perceived dishonorable. After his death, his spirit would haunt the wild, bringing terror to all the creatures it came upon.

Worshiping Cernunnos

As he has a torc, you can get one yourself that's dedicated to him; it's basically a necklace made of metal. He is typically honored on Beltane, which is on May 1, or November 1 if you're in the Southern Hemisphere. You can offer him sacred plants like grains, juniper, ivy, oak, and mistletoe. You can also bring him antler sheds, milk, soil, water, and wine. You can drum for him or perform sexual acts in his honor.

Cailleach

Cailleach is "the Veiled One." This goddess is in charge of winter and the winds and is often depicted as an old woman wearing a veil, sometimes having only one eye. Her skin is a shade of blue sometimes, though, at other times, it's incredibly pale. She has red teeth, and her dress is covered in skulls. She has both creative and destructive aspects, and she is the patron deity of wolves. Sometimes she is considered benevolent, and sometimes she's not to be messed around with because she's fearsome. While Brigid rules the summer, Cailleach is the goddess of winter. She had several marriages, but the most popular partner she ever had was Bodach, a trickster god with whom she had a lot of offspring.

The Queen of Winter determines how bad and long the winter gets. She was honored in the Isle of Man, Ireland, and Scotland, which are also her dwelling places. Cailleach translates to "hag" or "old woman" in Irish Gaelic and Scottish. She is also known as Birog, the fairy woman, Milucra, Bui (married to Lugh), Digde, Digdi, and Burach. The many names make some believe that she is a combination of several deities with similar traits.

The Veiled One can ride the storm, and she is so powerful that she can move over mountains in a single leap. She also has shape-shifting abilities. She has a hammer which she uses to create the new and destroy the old, and according to lore, she has power over thunder and storms. Sometimes she would wield her power over wells, making them overflow and destroy the land. You can't consider her a good or bad deity because, depending on the tale, she can be benevolent or malevolent. While she can be destructive, she has an unparalleled love for all animals, especially when the winter gets intense. She takes care of them.

This goddess is young, old, ageless, and immortal. When spring comes, she takes a draught that makes her young again. The Manx holds that she spends half the year as an old crone and the other half as a young maiden. So, she's known as Cailleach in the latter part of the year. According to the Irish, she had seven distinct periods when she was youthful, and after that, she remained old indefinitely.

Worshiping Cailleach

Cailleach doesn't need your worship, but if you want to honor her, you can simply spend time around mountains, caves, hills, rock formations, and other land formations. You can also spend time around natural bodies of water like whirlpools, rivers, and natural wells.

Cerridwen

She is the goddess of transformation, and she is also the ruler of knowledge and inspiration. Her name means "white crafty one" or "white sow." She is also known as the Grain Goddess, Nature Goddess, White Lady of Inspiration and Death, and the Dark Moon Goddess. She oversees magic, regeneration, death, and fertility. She rules the underworld, and her cauldron has the powers of rebirth, knowledge, and inspiration. She shows up in the lore surrounding Bran the Blessed, leaving her place in Ireland to dwell in the Land of the Mighty. She put on the disguise of Kymideu Kymeinvoll, a giantess, and she showed up with Llassar, her husband.

They both came out of a lake, which is essentially thought of as the underworld. The people feared the power they wielded, so they banished them. Bran offered the two of them safe harbor. All he wanted in return was Ceriddwen's cauldron, which could reanimate dead warriors whose bodies were put into it. Bran would eventually give Matholuch this cauldron during his marriage to Branwen, his sister. Cerridwen's cauldron combines the three known kinds of cauldrons: Transformation, Rebirth, and Inspiration.

Cerridwen is responsible for bringing life into the world and always cooking up something in her cauldron. She is the spiritual representation of the wheel of life, which includes birth, death, and rebirth cycles. She's the one to call on when you would like some growth in terms of your spirituality or some good luck in your physical life. She can also bring you abundance and nurture you. Small wonder then that her color is green, the very color of nature, which is abundant and gives freely to one and all.

Worshiping Cerridwen

To honor this goddess, you can offer her pork, acorns, vervain, grains, and other cereals. You should also work with your cauldron in her honor. You can find ways to incorporate the symbols that represent her, such as the dark moon, which represents her dark connection to magic, the moon in its various phases, and the white sow.

Herne

Also known as Herne the Hunter, he is considered a specter than a deity. He was responsible for putting man and animals through torment, and before you saw this antlered being, you would hear chains rattling and voices moaning. Some consider him to have been one of the aspects of Cernunnos. He would haunt the Berkshire woods often and always showed up on a mighty steed. Herne had a tree in Windsor Forest, his favorite haunt, known as Herne's Oak.

When it comes to his powers, he can make the natural world decay. All he needs to do is touch a finger to a tree, which would shrivel and die. He could also cause cattle to give blood rather than milk. According to folklore, he had a horn and would often travel in the company of hounds. When he shows up, it's believed something terrible is about to happen. He's a very mysterious deity, mostly because he rarely interacts with anyone when he encounters people. What is sure, though, is that his energy is cruel, and it could be because of how he died — by taking his own life.

Some believe that Herne was related to the Norse god of the dead, Odin. Odin is synonymous with Wotan and was in charge of the Wild Hunt, a quest to rally souls that had passed on for his army of the dead. Herne became popular during the Victorian era, just like the Baphomet, a horned god, and demon. He is a common god for English neopagan movements.

Worshiping Herne

You can offer this god some whiskey, cider, and mead. You can also offer him some meat. If you hunted the meat yourself, it's even better. Try burning some incense for him, especially the kind with dried autumn leaves. He considers this smoke sacred, and you can use it to send your requests to him so that he can give you a speedy response.

Lugh

He's the god of justice. He's the one who ensures oaths are kept and is also in charge of nobility. This god is considered a trickster god with the capacity to save those in trouble. He is well known for his successful war tactics and his excellent craftsmanship. Not only is he considered a warrior king, but he's also a hero to the Irish. His wife had a lover named Cermait, whose three sons would kill him by driving a spear through his foot and then drowning him. This was in response to his killing of Cermait. Lugh had the legendary Spear of Assal, and it was near impossible for anyone to escape being hurt by that weapon when he wielded it against them.

Sometimes, Lugh is also known as Lug, and it is hypothesized that the name comes from Proto-Indo-European roots, from the word *lewgh,* which means "to bind by oath." This makes sense because Lugh was particular about contracts being honored to the letter. Some say the name means "light," but no one is completely sure. He made sure that justice was served, and he would execute judgment with speed and with no room for reconsideration. Yet, he also had a penchant for being a trickster. This meant he had no problem stealing, lying, and cheating to ensure he had the upper hand over his enemies.

Worshiping Lugh

Lugh is worshiped on Lughnasa, also known as Lughnasadh. This Irish festival is held on August 1, celebrated in the Isle of Man, Ireland, and Scotland. It's a significant day because it was when Lugh triumphed over the Tir na nOg spirits. To mark this occasion, he granted an early harvest of fruits and honored his Tailtiu, his foster mother, by hosting some games. This day is also known in Christianity as Mountain Sunday or Garland Sunday. You can offer him bread, grains, corn, and anything else that represents the idea of harvest.

Morrigan

This Irish goddess is in charge of destiny, battle, and death. She has three aspects to her, all sisters, and can also show up as just one being. She rules fate and is in charge of the gift of prophecy. No matter who approached her, whether a deity or a hero, she would do them favors and offer them prophecy. You can see her as a raven flying around a battlefield, waiting for the carrion she can eat and take away. She also had the power of shapeshifting; whenever she showed up, it was considered a terrible omen because someone was sure to die. Sometimes, you'll hear her or them referred to as "The Morrigan." She is also known as the Great Queen or the Phantom Queen.

This prophetess can show up not just like a raven but as an old crone, a young, beautiful maiden, and a warrior queen with fierceness in her gaze. Since she is connected to fate and prophecy, it's not unusual to learn that she's connected to the death of mighty individuals. She showed up as a raven on Ulster as he died. She also shows up as a washerwoman with something strange and otherworldly about her. In this case, you'll find her bloody and washing clothes that belonged to those who have passed on in battle.

This is a goddess with three aspects. Depending on who you ask, their individual names are Badb, Macha, and Nemain. Other times, Nemain is known as Dannan, Danu, Anand, or Anu. It is Badb that shows up as a raven during battle. Note that each aspect or sister can act on her own. Nemain and Badb have a thing for giving deathly screeches so terrifying that at least 100 men who hear them at night die because they're frightened, and with good reason. That shriek means terrible things to come, and their deaths could well be considered merciful compared to the onslaught they would have otherwise witnessed.

Worshiping the Morrigan

It's a good idea to leave her offerings regularly, as the more you do, the more power you generate for your rituals. Craft a separate altar for her if you can. If not, create a space just for her on your altar. You can offer her stormwater, red wine, red foods, honey, mead, milk, a boline knife, feathers from a crow, poetry, art, and foods native to Ireland.

You can offer red wine to Morrigan.
https://pixabay.com/images/id-541922/

Chapter 4: Hedge Riding and the Other World

Hedge riding is also known as hedge jumping or hedge flying. This skill is necessary if you're going to be a hedge witch, but what is it exactly? The word "hedge" can take on various connotations in hedge witchcraft, and one of them is the boundary that separates this physical world from the spiritual one, otherwise known as the Otherworld. The hedge acts to keep humans and spirits apart from each other. When you hear of a hedge witch "riding the hedge" or "flying the hedge," what's going on is the witch is crossing over, going through the veil from the physical world to the spirit world.

So, hedge riding is taking a spiritual trip into the realm of spirit, where the collective unconscious lies. This act is shamanic, reminiscent of traveling to the astral realm. In other words, it's pretty much the same thing as astral projection. Usually, it's something you do on your own as a hedge witch, although some witches like to work together to have more insight and value to share from their journeys. You can perform rituals and spells as a group in the Otherworld if that's what you'd like to do. The good thing about riding the hedge with others is that you can have someone else's perspective on things, which could help you consider matters you may not have thought about.

Hedge Riding, Shamanic Travels, and Astral Projection

The difference between hedge riding and shamanic travels is that the witch isn't getting into psychopomp affairs. She doesn't help souls to move on to their next journey. Instead, she travels to gain insight and knowledge, heal, and practice divination, meditation, and her craft. Hedge riding is also different from shamanic travels because the hedge witch doesn't seek to control her journey. Instead, she goes along with the ride and doesn't attempt to control what happens next. She is, however, in charge of her actions. While astral projection often happens in our own level of existence (as well as several others), hedge riding is meant to get you to the Otherworld itself.

To be clear, hedge riding isn't a function of visualization or imagination. It is the actual process of leaving the physical world. You have to keep in mind that you don't control the journey you experience. If you aren't careful and respectful of the process, you may encounter dangerous forces that could cause you harm.

Before you can hedge ride, you must enter a state of altered consciousness. There are many ways to do this, such as chanting, meditation, dancing, drumming, and even taking certain psychedelic medicines. It's much better not to use drugs as a pathway to altered consciousness because you may encounter more danger as you cannot control yourself. However, in the past, the hedge witch used magical ointments to help her transition from the physical world to the Otherworld by inducing a state of altered consciousness.

The Otherworld and Hedge Riding

There are three distinct aspects to the Otherworld; the Upper, Middle, and Lower realms. Each of these worlds has nine levels. One form of this world is the Yggdrasil, the World Tree of Norse mythology. Now let's talk about the Havamal, a collection of verses in the 13th century Poetic Edda. The 156th verse has two translations and talks about the process of flying the hedge. You can use either translation of this verse to make the hedge rider reveal who they truly are, head back to their home, or keep their spirit apart from their body. The bottom line is that it's clear from these verses that hedge riding is an actual practice and that often, travelers take on a form different from their physical one. The better you get at hedge riding, the more you'll be able to shape-shift into different creatures to stay safe. Usually, the hedge rider will travel with animal guides to keep themselves safe and guide them along their journey through worlds unknown.

This is a dangerous practice only if you allow yourself to be overwhelmed with fear, an energy that will draw negative entities to you. You must recognize that you have every right to travel to the Otherworld and that you're a sovereign being with autonomy over yourself. If you don't, trickster spirits and malevolent entities could take advantage of you. This is why taking precautions before you fly the hedge is important. You shouldn't be afraid because there's a lot of good to be experienced from the Otherworld that makes the process worth it for you as a hedge witch. Let's look at some rituals you can perform before crossing to Otherworld.

Cleansing Ritual

It is good practice to cleanse yourself and your space often, especially when you intend to work with spirits or cross over the hedge. Cleansing also ensures that they don't attach themselves to you or your space when you've finished working with the spirits. If you don't, you may notice that the energy in your home feels wrong and is even kind of heavy. Also, you may have a difficult time flying the hedge. So, you must begin cleansing to raise the vibrations of your space and your being. You can do routine cleanses but note that sometimes you need to go deeper because there are places where energy remains trapped, for example, in a closet that is often shut or a room you hardly go into. So now and then, get deep into cleansing.

You'll Need:

- 4 quartz crystals
- 3 amethyst crystals
- 1 malachite crystal
- 1 small white candle
- A picture or carving of a coyote (other scavenger animals like a vulture or raccoon will do as well)
- A bundle of sage
- 5 sage leaves (fresh or dried)
- 3 sprigs of rosemary (fresh or dried)

- Salt
- A broom
- Saltwater in a bowl
- Lighter or matches

Steps:
1. Clean your home from top to bottom, ensuring you don't neglect any spot. This means moving your furniture to get underneath it, opening closets and rooms to let them get air and light, removing all cobwebs, and so on. The idea is to stimulate the flow of energy. If you can't find the time or your home is properly cleaned and organized already, focus on removing dust from the floor.
2. After cleaning, move around your home from room to room and clap your hands. If there's somewhere you don't often go, clap there. Also, clap behind doors, beneath the couch and other furniture, and in corners of the rooms. This will awaken the energy there.
3. Next, set up your altar in a central location in your home, like the kitchen or your living room. Make sure it's not on the floor and has enough space to put all the items you'll be working with on it. Also, make sure it's in a space that will let you cast a circle of salt around it.
4. The image or carving of the coyote should be placed centrally onto your altar and a candle placed above or behind it.
5. Put the quartz crystals at each corner, ensuring they face outward.
6. Put the malachite to the south of the carving.
7. Place the amethyst in the other cardinal directions.
8. Put your sage leaves next to your quartz crystals.
9. Put one sprig of rosemary on the left and the other on the right (East and West).
10. Get your salt and create a circle all around the altar.
11. Now, it's time for you to invoke the spirit you seek to talk to. Say a short prayer to it, asking for its help with the cleansing ritual.
12. Next, light the candle, then proclaim that the candle's energy now purifies your home.

13. Now it's time to spread salt all over your floors. If they're carpeted, please use baking soda instead. You should make sure the salt gets everywhere.
14. When you've finished salting your floor, you should begin vacuuming or sweeping, moving from the Northwest direction to the Southeast while chanting that your home is now being swept clean of negative energy and that only love and joy fill it.
15. You'll have a heap of salt when you've finished. Flush it down the toilet, envisioning the negative energy going down the drain. If it's too much to flush, throw it in the garbage outside the home.
16. Take your other sage leaf and rosemary sprig and put it in your salt water. Use the rosemary sprig to sprinkle the water around your space in a counterclockwise motion. As you do this, say a short prayer affirming that you cleanse your home with water and earth and that only love and joy fill your home.
17. Light the sage and use the smoke to cleanse your space, working counterclockwise as you say a short prayer affirming you cleanse your home with air and fire, and only love and joy fill your home.
18. Meditate for about five minutes before your altar, noting the light feeling in your space when you've finished. Let the candle burn down, and thank your spirit for its assistance. When you've finished, take a bath to rid yourself of any negativity.

Protection Ritual

Protection is a matter of mindset. You need to realize nothing can harm you without your permission, and you grant permission to be harmed by being afraid or expecting to be hurt. You must remain unfazed by whatever you encounter as you hedge ride. However, a simple practice you can do is imagine yourself being surrounded by golden light. Picture this light as an eggshell around you, keeping everything and anyone who means you harm away from you. You can make it as big or bright as you want. As you're in the Otherworld, it will show up around you and effectively keep you safe.

Grounding Ritual

1. Plant your feet firmly on the ground.
2. Imagine your feet growing roots into the core of the Earth.

3. Feel yourself taking in the Earth's energy through the soles of your feet from the earth up and through the rest of your body.
4. Breathe deeply for a minute or more as you feel the energy flowing through you. You will notice that you feel calmer and more present. When you do, you'll know you've done it right.

How to Hedge Ride

To let your spirit separate from your body, you have to alter your state of consciousness. You can do this naturally or through induction. Please avoid using drugs to help you ride the hedge. Here are safer methods to alter your consciousness:

Shamanic drumming works well; you can find many videos on YouTube to help you. There's a start and an ending to the tracks to help you leave this world and gently bring you back to it. Before you use them, you should listen to what they sound like so you know the signal to return to your body. You should limit your ride to 15 minutes initially, and then you can work your way up.

Shamanic music is like drumming, but there are other sounds like chants and rattles. This may not work well for you if you don't like voices.

Rattling is another form of music you can find on YouTube, but it's often better for you to use the rattle to generate the sound. It helps if you sway your body in time with the beat.

Dancing is another method for altering your consciousness, but it's not the easiest, and you can tire easily. The idea is that you must dance until you can no longer remain on your feet. This is ideal when you're dancing around a fire outside or in a warm room with dim lights. If you choose this method, you should have music and chanting to make things go smoothly.

Chanting is similar in effect to drumming and rattling. You can either listen to chants on YouTube or chant on your own. It's often best to work some other action into chanting, like clapping.

Listening to your heartbeat is another option because your heart is basically a biological drum. The room you're in has to be quiet. Take a seat or lie down and then listen to it. You can plug your ears if it helps you hear them better.

Goals

It's a good idea to aim for entering the Lower Realm first. To do this, state your intention to go there out loud. Then repeat the intention in your head over and over again. Then, when you've got that fixed in your head, choose your method for altering your consciousness, and surrender yourself to the process.

When you want to enter the Otherworld, you've got to cross the veil, also known as the hedge. This is a portal, which looks different for every hedge witch. It could be anything from a mirror to a hollowed-out tree trunk. You can bring this image to your mind as you practice your altered state of consciousness technique so that you'll see the portal before you when you switch consciousness.

Go through the portal into a tunnel, which can look like anything, from a hallway of doors to an actual tunnel. If you're going to the Lower Realms, the tunnel should head downwards. The tunnel should be flat when going to the Middle Realms, and the Upper Realms should have a tunnel that leads upward. Keep walking until you finally make your way toward the other side, where there should be light. Please note that this may not happen the very first time you try it. If it doesn't, don't beat yourself up. Just try the next day and the day after that again. Eventually, you will pierce the veil. When you're ready to come back, do so the same way you did.

Ideally, you should get used to the Lower Realms first before you start traveling elsewhere. This is the safest place for you to explore, and when you meet your guides and are familiar with them, you can then move on to the Middle Realms, then the Upper Realms. Please don't set any expectations for yourself so you're not disappointed. As you gain more experience, you will have more interesting journeys. If you have trouble piercing the veil, you may have issues with self-doubt. You need to allow yourself to believe that you can do this and then try again.

Meditation and Deities

Meditation helps you remain grounded and connects you to the deities.
https://www.pexels.com/photo/peaceful-lady-sitting-in-padmasana-pose-while-meditating-on-mat-4498220/

You should be able to work with the deities if you're having difficulty. Just ask for their help by offering them or meditating on them, so you can soak in their energies. Meditation is also a great practice because it helps you remain grounded, which you need when riding the hedge. You can also work with your spirit allies. Who are they? Let's talk about that in the next chapter.

Chapter 5: Spirit Allies and How to Find Them

In this life, you never walk alone. You have a team of supporters who are always with you, regardless of what's happening. You may not be able to see them all the time, but that doesn't mean they're not there. These are your spirit guides or spirit allies. Some beings are devoted to helping you through your life. Your spirit guide(s) could be a power animal, angel, fairy, ancestor, elemental, or entire divine councils.

One important thing to note about your spirit guides is that they must adhere to universal laws. In other words, as much as they may want to help you through a particular situation, they can't interfere unless and until you reach out to them for help. In other words, they are respecters of free will. Your spirit guide is eternally devoted to your highest good. They're there to ensure that you fulfill your soul's calling before you incarnated up on this planet. They're always there to make things easier for you.

Full of compassion and eager to help you, they are in charge of helping to wake you up from the illusion of "real" life. They wake you up to your greatness, so you can see there is no reason to kowtow to the troubles you've been burdened with since you were born. They help you awaken to your innate divinity, showing you areas where you have blind spots. They can teach you the correct attitude to have and help you deal with the daily fears you face. It is well worth it to take some time to learn who your spirit guides are and how they can be of assistance to you. As you do this, you will quickly realize that life doesn't have to be difficult.

Your spirit guide's job is to bring you to places and things that will help you along your journey. They will show you where you're struggling that you may not be aware of and how to break through this struggle. While they are full of love and compassion, they do not have any trouble doing what needs to be done to bring you to where you need to be. They will do everything necessary to make you stop telling the stories you continue to use to imprison yourself in your undesired version of reality. They do this because when you become conscious of who you are, there is nothing that could hold you back from achieving whatever you want in life.

How Your Guides Show Up

Sometimes your spirit guides will reveal themselves in this physical world as very strong supporters of your cause or as people who are incredibly difficult and challenging to deal with. When they show up as the latter, it basically forces you to come face to face with your shadow aspects to heal and integrate them, so you can move on to the next level in life. That very difficult person you're dealing with could be your boss, for instance. Say they continue to assign you duties outside your job description, refuse to give you a raise, or unjustly cut your pay. It's easy to get mad, but there's no reason to. They may not be conscious of this, but your guide could be using them and their constant pushes against you to wake you up to the prison you've constructed and consented to. They could show you it's time to start something new or devote yourself completely to your own business. Your guide could also be working through a lover, showing you the stories you've come to accept about your lack of worth, so you can finally learn that you do deserve love, fully and truly. They can use anyone and any situation to get through to you. You just have to pay attention.

Types of Spirit Guides and How to Connect with Them

Ancestors

These are spirit guides you share a connection with through your physical or spiritual lineage. They could also be some of the people you've known and loved who have passed on to their next life and are now offering you guidance from their higher perspective. It is more common to have your ancestors come from many generations back. They could be a great-grandfather or someone with spiritual gifts who was your former incarnation.

Ancestors are never stingy with their support and guidance. Whether you have limiting beliefs that need to be taken care of or trauma that you need to let go of, they will be there to help you. They can bring your attention to wounds you may have neglected for far too long so you can finally heal them. Sometimes very specific traumas pass on from one generation to the next, which could need healing in your present incarnation. They are also on hand to help you finally help your lineage break free. They can act as teachers, showing you who you really are, and revealing the gifts you may not be aware of so you can use them to live life to the fullest.

How to Connect with Ancestors

1. **Connect with Them through Meditation:** Find a quiet, still space in your home. It can simply be a room where you sit, close your eyes, and meditate. Sit and state your intention to connect with your ancestors out loud, and then keep that intention fixed in your mind while you focus on your breath. Visualize a white light emanating from the top of your head and filling the entire room. Keep this up till you feel the energy shift. This will connect you. From this state, you could let them know what you want them to help you with, express your appreciation for all they've done for you so far, or just let them know you'd like to have a deeper, more meaningful relationship with them.

2. **Start Connecting with Your Elders before They Pass On**: Try to create deep connections with them before they leave this plane, and it will be easier for you to connect with them when they're on the other side in a position to help you more than they possibly could on this side. Don't connect with them only for selfish reasons. Truly be there for them and show them how much you care. They will return the favor from the other side.

3. **Honor Your Family Traditions**: Try to find ways to honor your ancestors. This means participating in some of the traditions you have, whether it be gathering together for family dinners or taking a few moments in your day to say thank you for their advice and wisdom.

4. **Develop a Habit of Speaking to Them Daily:** There is a reason why they want you to connect with them daily. They want to remind you of who you are and help you live your best life by passing on their wisdom, guidance, and teachings. Listen to their

call. You want communion with them, which means listening to them, not just talking to them. This way, they will reveal themselves in your life with purpose. But don't be disappointed if they don't always respond right away. Trust that they will, and when the time is right, in a way that works out beautifully for you.

Angels

An angel can be described as a "spirit guide on steroids." They are much more powerful and able to help you in a way that other spirits may not be able to. These beings are of the highest spiritual light and have been here from the beginning of time. The angels are here to help you achieve your highest potential. They help you connect to your spirit, and they can send your messages to the higher realms, making sure they are received. They can help you get into a state of being that is more inspiring than where you're at right now.

Angels are benevolent spiritual beings that help you on your journey. They are not here to judge you; they guide, protect, and heal your soul. They have pure intentions and will not steer you in the wrong direction with what they teach. Angels bring their pure love and light energy in to help you do the things that help guide and assist in your spiritual development.

How to Connect with Angels

1. **Connect with Them through the Act of Prayer:** Prayer is the most common way to connect with your angels. Praying to the angels helps you align your energy with theirs and opens a loving line of communication for when you need them. You can pray for guidance, protection, healing, help with any obstacles in your life, or anything else that's troubling you. A good angel guide to pray to would be Archangel Michael, who is known as the warrior of angelic light and who serves as a mentor to help you in times of trouble.

2. **Notice Intense Sensations and Emotions That Hit You from Nowhere:** These can be flashes of light, a tingling sensation in your body, a sudden wave of energy in your stomach, or any other physical sensation. Your angels may also send you thoughts from out of nowhere.

3. **Intend to Connect with Them in Your Dreams**: You can do this by setting the intention in meditation to connect with your angels

during your dream. You can also ask them to help you remember some of your dreams so that you can better understand what they are trying to tell you.
4. **Create a Sacred Space in Your Home**: This is an area where you feel safe, protected, and inspired to connect with higher spiritual beings freely.

Star Beings

Other-dimensional beings heavily influence human life. The star beings have a lot to do with how humanity is today and have helped us get this far regarding our physical and spiritual evolution. You can think of them as our spirit guides from other dimensions, some of whom we know from our past on other planets or in other universes, and others from our future. They have helped us expand our consciousness so we can start to get in touch with other dimensions and beyond.

Star beings are not exactly angels, but they possess similar traits. They also have a lot of knowledge of the future. Their role is to help us further expand our understanding of creation and give us a sense of hope that we will make it through any obstacle or challenge that happens in our life with blessings from other dimensions. The star beings bring higher ideas and notions to Earth and influence how we see things from an entirely new perspective that helps us understand our own spirituality, purpose, and many other factors in life.

How to Connect with Star Beings

1. **Fly the Hedge to Connect with Them:** Each time you fly the hedge, you can set an intention to meet with them or speak with them. You may not do so on the first try, but with patience and with persistence, you'll be able to connect with them. This is because you will have adjusted your vibration to a state where it's easy to connect with them. Note that when you communicate with each other, it will likely be through telepathy. You may experience a phenomenon where you're getting "downloads" of information, which is a much more effective way of getting messages across than with words.
2. **Spend Time Star Gazing:** Observing the stars and other celestial bodies is a great way to connect with higher dimensions. Doing so helps expand your consciousness and gives you a sense of calm and internal peace.

Stargazing helps you connect with star beings.
https://pixabay.com/images/id-1851128/

1. **Meditate:** Through meditating, you work on clearing your mind of any negativity or clutter that may be hindering your ability to connect with star beings. This helps you raise your vibration and get in the right state to connect with them. You may hear their messages through your dreams or just get a general sense of guidance, inspiration, or peace while meditating.

2. **Connect with Them through Crystals:** Crystals have a high concentration of energy that connects with higher dimensions. They can help you connect with the star beings and other spirit guides and allies.

Ascended Masters

They are human beings who incarnated in a past life on Earth to help and teach us along our path. In some cases, they may have incarnated multiple times, but their purpose, for now, is to teach you something, help you with a specific task, or just be there as support for you. Ascended masters may be from other planets or other universes, or they could have been human beings (from Earth) who ascended beyond and experienced countless lifetimes of a tremendous amount of spiritual development throughout many lifetimes.

The ascended masters have spiritually evolved beings who have reached a point of enlightenment, where they are spiritually developed to the point they no longer need reincarnation. They may choose to come back to Earth as an ascended master and help us with our spiritual growth, but the ascension is such that they don't need to experience the suffering and pain of physical life. Some will travel throughout the universe, and others will stay in lower dimensions, but all of them are here on Earth as ascended masters and spirit guides.

How to Connect with Ascended Masters

1. **Open Your Heart to Them:** The ascended masters have reached a point of having an open heart, able to love unconditionally. So, to connect with ascended masters, you need to open your heart to the world. You need to love unconditionally, care for others without putting conditions on them, and get past the fear of being hurt or vulnerable. As you open your heart further, more and more ascended masters will come into your life.

2. **Ask for Help from Ascended Masters:** The ascended masters are compassionate, kind, and selfless beings who are willing to come and help you if you ask them. When you ask for their help, you need to be respectful that their time is precious - just as yours is. If you're asking for guidance on a task or problem in your life, be specific about what you want and respect their time - don't waste it.

3. **Pay Attention to Signs in Your Life:** As you open your heart to others and ask for help, you will begin to see signs and messages from them in the most unlikely places. These signs can be as simple as seeing a butterfly or an owl in a strange place in a strange time or hearing something that reminds you of your goal. Sometimes people report hearing their name being whispered when nobody is around. Some people have reported seeing an image of themselves from the future because they can connect with their future self using their higher intuition.

4. **Meditate on Your Higher Self:** You may find connecting with your higher self easier than the masters. You may also be closer to what is your higher self than even spiritual masters or angels since your higher self is the most evolved form of yourself and is closer to God. When you meditate on your higher self, you can ask it to put you in touch with the masters if you want, and it will be easier.

Animal Spirit Guides

Animal spirit guides are spiritual or angelic beings that can take many animal forms and are an extension of yourself. You're meant to connect with them and the Divine through them. Like ascended masters, animal spirit guides may have incarnated in a past life on Earth for a reason, but in this time, they work with you to help you awaken spiritually.

These are animal guides who have been with us since birth. Although they may not seem like much, they are extremely powerful, intelligent, and wise beings who can teach you many things about yourself. Who we are as human beings is a combination of our personality and our animal spirit guides.

How to Connect with Animal Spirit Guides

1. **Connect with Your Senses:** Animals are very in touch with their senses, and so it makes sense that you connect with yours if you want to relate to them. So, practice really looking around, taking in everything around you. Notice what you can hear and the different qualities in each sound. Pay attention to what you can smell, feel, and taste. Work with each sense one at a time for five minutes a day.

2. **Get a Talisman That Represents the Animal You're Most Drawn to:** A talisman is an object that has a spiritual significance. You can carry your talisman with you everywhere and connect with it whenever you're having trouble. Talismans are medallions or objects which have been charged with the energy of a specific time and place, as well as being imbued with the universal energy of creation. To charge your talisman, you can meditate on your preferred animal while you hold the talisman in your hands and set an intention so that, as you carry it around with you, you have the guidance, protection, and assistance of your spirit animal wherever you are.

3. **Connect with Them in Your Dreams:** Our dreams are the best place to reconnect with our animal spirit guides. These beings are very powerful in dreams, and some report having lucid dreams or daydreaming about them. All you have to do is set the intention to meet with them as you go to sleep.

4. **Ask Them for Help:** You can ask your animal spirit guides for anything. This is a great way to learn more about yourself and

discover your purpose on Earth. Don't be surprised if you start seeing or hearing about that animal more often when you reach out for help. When they show up, they're trying to tell you everything will be okay and that they are working on what you want.

Deities

We've already talked about some deities particular to hedge witchcraft and Celtic lore. You can connect with anyone you resonate with, and they will answer you. Just make sure to be respectful of them and their time and be sincere in whatever you want to ask for their assistance.

How to Connect with Deities

1. **Make Offerings to Them:** You know what it is they like. Offer it to them by setting it on your altar.
2. **Set Their Image around Your Space:** You can have pictures of your deities in your home or around your spiritual workspace. Each time you see the picture, take a moment to say hello in your mind, thank them, or just acknowledge them however you can.
3. **Light a Candle in Their Honor:** If you're feeling lost, depressed, anxious, or even very happy because something good happened, you can light a candle to acknowledge them. This practice will fill your home and life with their energy.
4. **Meditate on Them:** You can chant their name repeatedly as you meditate, either aloud or in your mind. As you do this, you'll feel your body and heart filled with their energy. That tells you that they're present with you.

Elemental Spirit Guides

Elementals are spirits that you find in one of the four classical elements: Earth, water, fire, and air. Not all of them are allies, but the ones who are can be considered guides. Gnomes are earth elementals, undines are connected to water, pyraustas are also known as salamanders, and they're connected to fire, while sylphs are connected to water. Generally, these elementals will make their home in the elements themselves, like rocks, mountains, bodies of water, fire, and the wind.

How to Connect with Elemental Spirit Guides

1. **Spend Time in Nature:** The more you are out in nature, the more you'll be able to connect with them.
2. **Start Caring for the Planet:** You can do this by becoming more conscious about your habits and practices that don't do our earth any favors. You can also do little things like getting rid of litter, raking leaves, etc. As you do these things, keep the elements in your mind.
3. **Intend to Connect with Them:** This is easy to do when you're working with a specific element. Air is all around you, so you should have no problem with that. It might help to go camping or at least light a candle for fire. For water, you can work with a bowl full of it. As for the earth, sand or salt will do.
4. **Carry around the Element You Want to Work With:** It can be a bit trickier for fire and air, but for the former, you can just use a lighter or a match. For the latter, becoming conscious of the air you're breathing will do the trick.

The Aos Si

These are like elves or fairies, coming from the Tuatha Dé Danann. They make their home underground in a world that, while invisible, exists right along with ours. They are immortal, and they can help you in life as well. Some people call them The Fair Folk, while others call them The Good Neighbors, and they are exactly that. They can be as hideous as they are stunning in how they look. They act as guardians, fiercely protective of those they consider theirs.

How to Connect with the Aos Si

1. **Fly the Hedge:** This is a good way to reach them, as they're essentially inhabitants of the Otherworld.
2. **Meditate on Them at Dawn and Dusk:** These are the two periods when the veil between worlds is thinnest, and therefore you should find it easier to connect with them and let them know what you need them to help with.
3. **Celebrate Their Holidays:** Now's a good time to get familiar with Midsummer, Beltane, and Samhain. These are the three festivals with which they are most associated. You can work with fellow hedge witches to make them group offerings. The combined

energies will prove to be fruitful, regardless of what you seek from them.
4. **Offer Them Foods Regularly:** Berries, apples, milk, and other baked goods are a favorite for the Good Neighbors.

Chapter 6: Magical Herbs, Plants, and Trees

In this chapter, we'll talk about the magical herbs, plants, and trees you can work with in your craft. You can easily pick up all these herbs from your grocery store or a store that sells items for witchcraft. You can also find them online, fresh or dried, so there's no need to be obsessed with scouting around your neighborhood looking for them unless that's something you like to do.

Magical Herbs

Mint: It's kind of odd to have mint included as a magical herb to some witches, but the truth is that it is powerful and deserves to be mentioned. This herb can give you energy and add power to your rituals and spells. It will help you clear your mind and set intentions to bring proper results. It also awakens your senses, which is always good for magical work. You can drink it as tea, eat it, or just smell it to prime yourself to do your spells successfully. This herb can also draw success and money to you, and it's good for drumming up business. Good spirits are attracted to it, and it keeps your home safe from negative energies and entities.

Thyme: This herb is popular in various spells because it has so many intriguing properties and uses. You can use thyme if you want to speak with the dead and connect with them. It's also good for consecrating rituals and keeping your spells aligned with your intentions. You can wear it to ward off snakes and spiders, keep it around the house to protect your family from illness, or add a bit of thyme to your bath water for a relaxing soak. Be sure that you're planting organic thyme, though. No one wants pesticides in their "magical" herb garden.

Bay Leaf: You can use this leaf to hold divine energy. It's a very versatile herb and works for various types of spells and magical workings. If you're trying to cleanse your aura, wear it in a pendant or amulet. If you want to ask your deity to bless you, you can burn its leaves in incense. It will also help you with spells that involve protection, luck, and prosperity because it's an herb of abundance. It is especially useful in protection and cleansing rites. It's a good herb for removing negative entities and cleansing your space. You can use the bay leaf in your bath water to cleanse yourself of "negative energies." Bay leaves are also great for drawing good luck and attracting prosperity.

Rosemary: Rosemary is one of the oldest herbs on earth, and its scent is magnificent. You can use it in incense for purification and blessings. Burning it is also a great way to attract good energy into your home or workplace. Rosemary is a very versatile herb, and it's good for healing in various ways. It's also a potent herb for protection magic, and its scent adds an energy vibration that can help you focus your intent. Burning rosemary at night will keep the evil spirits away from you and your family. You can also rub the leaves on your body to prevent illness or add some sprigs to your bath water for a relaxing soak.

Rosemary attracts healing.
https://pixabay.com/images/id-1140763/

Lavender: Lavender is a lovely smelling herb that has many magical uses. You can use it to cleanse yourself before entering a sacred space or performing magic. It's also good for ritual work and as a repellent for unwanted spirits. It can remove negative energy or change its vibration. Burn it in an incense burner for attraction magic, or sprinkle some around your house to repel unwanted entities. Wear it in jewelry, put some on the bottom of your feet before you go out, leave a bundle under your bed, or place a lavender sachet in your car, so you'll be protected as you go about town.

Oregano: These leaves are great for drawing good luck and attracting prosperity. They stimulate the senses and clear the mind so you can set proper intentions. Add some to salads or put a few pinches in your ritual bath. Oregano is also used in shamanic practices to help you connect with the spirit world. During ritual work, burn it in an incense burner or grind a few leaves and add them to your bath water. You can also sprinkle it around your home for protection or wear it as an amulet for added safety when traveling.

Ginger Root: This herb is great for healing and exorcism. It can also help you stay focused during spell work and ritual work. It's a powerful blocker against negative thoughts and actions, so it helps you keep your intentions pure. When magical work is done around the house, burn some ginger in an incense burner or sachet to clear out the energy from the space, or wear it as a pendant to ward off negativity and attract good fortune. Ginger root is great for drawing; good luck to you. It's also wonderful for adding energy to many types of rituals, spells, and magic work, as it acts as a magical accelerant. It's great for banishing spirits and removing negative energy from your space. Ginger root will also lift your spirits and help you feel more energetic during your spells and rituals.

Fennel Seed: Fennel seed is a powerful herb used in ritual work. It has a sweet scent that acts as a stimulant for the mind, so you can use it in spells to keep you focused on your intentions. This herb is also very good for purification magic because it cleanses the aura of negative energy, which is good for any spell or ritual that involves protection, health, or cleanliness issues.

Allspice: This is another herb that witches can use in many rituals. It is an excellent purifying agent, is used against negativity, and helps you communicate with the dead. The smell is reminiscent of clove and cinnamon, and the taste also hints of black pepper. It's a very popular addition to feast offerings to the gods and goddesses. Allspice can be used in any magic, from blessing rituals to protection magic. It is also considered a sacred herb by many cultures. You can use it in spells involving love, money, and fertility.

Dandelion: Dandelion is one of the most popular magical herbs because it's both easy and inexpensive to obtain. The root is used in magical arts to remove negativity, while the leaves and flowers attract abundance. You can also use this herb during spells that involve home protection, luck, love, and purification. It's a very potent spell enhancer that improves the power of any spell or magic you perform with it. To attract money, burn dandelion on charcoal for your incense, or put some in a sachet for travel money or business earnings. Dandelion is a great herb that can be used as a tea, too. Traditionally, this herb is also used for healing. It's good to sprinkle it on the ground where you practice your craft or wear it as an amulet before entering your ritual area.

Magical Plants

Money Tree: This herb has so many desirable qualities that it's used in almost every type of magic, from blessing rituals to protection spells and love rituals. In some cultures, the leaves are used as an ingredient in lucky tea or herbal brews consumed to draw good fortune and prosperity. You can use it in any spell that brings good fortune or prosperity your way. Try pairing it with other herbs like ginger, cinnamon, or nutmeg for added effect.

Jade Plant: This plant represents abundance and energy. It is a good one to use when you want wisdom. You can make a protective sachet of jade and carry it with you as you travel to ward off unwanted energies. You can use jade to lift your spirits when feeling down or stressed. This plant is also good for clearing out negativity in the aura, so it's a great helper when working on spells that involve the mind or emotions. This is a magical herb that's used in rituals and spells involving psychic awareness, as well as healing properties. It is known to bring good luck and to help you achieve your goals. You can also use it in household cleansing spells.

Devil's Ivy: This herb is traditionally used in magic to attract prosperity, but it can also be used to draw luck. When you use devil's ivy, it brings goodwill and fortune and strengthens your powers of perception. Devil's ivy is also excellent for protecting your home or property. It's a good herb for making love potions or for healing spells. Devil's ivy has a very powerful scent that repels all the negative energy in the area. You can use it to purify your space or in protection and health spells. Wearing the plant as an amulet will help you ward off many types of negativity, including thoughts and physical harassment. Use this plant to give you resilience and to help you work spells that involve forgiveness.

English Ivy: This popular magical herb is used to protect magic, increase psychic powers, and promote goodwill. It's a very good one to use in spells involving cleansing and protection. You can also use it in spells that involve banishing negativity or evil. English ivy is easy to find, inexpensive, and easy to grow - all of which make this one of the most popular magical herbs around. You can use it in any type of protective or blessing spell. Because the scent is both sweet and fragrant, it's a good herb to banish negative thoughts and attract positive energy into your life.

Houseleek: This plant is a succulent one also called Hens and Chicks. It's underrated but powerful. The ancient Romans would decorate their homes with this plant. You can eat it, but only in small amounts. It's great if you want to deal with inflammation in the body. Use this plant to create good health in your life. It can also improve your family affairs, boost fertility in whatever aspect of life you need it, and keep you protected. This plant gives off a comforting aura, putting you at ease and turning anywhere it grows into a home. You can also use them to bring more sexual energy into the bedroom or with spells that involve love and sexuality.

Bamboo: This is a good herb to use for purification and protection magic. It represents money and sexuality. Bamboo can attract money, wealth, and power when burned as incense or used in spellwork. Bamboo represents resilience and flexibility. It also promotes peace and clarity and can bring you good luck. Bamboo's smooth branches are sometimes used for spiritual cleansing and meditation as a tool for divination. You can use it to attract happiness and health into your life. It is said that the more stalks of this plant you have, the more power and luck you can draw on for your craft.

Magical Trees

Alder: Many ancient people considered the alder tree to be sacred. It was used in many magical and religious rituals because it is so very powerful. This tree is beneficial for protection spells, cleansing rites, and healing magic. It's also used for banishing evil spirits and negative energies, and it can help you boost your psychic powers and strengthen your memory. You can use its parts for ritual work or spells involving the banishment of negativity, healing, meditation, and communication with spirits. Use it as part of a protective mojo bag or scatter some leaves around the area where you're doing your spell or ritual work so that the energy will feel welcoming and positive.

Beech: This tree is a wonderful source of spiritual energy because its wood has been used in making ritual tools since the Stone Age. It's used in divination and has been associated with gods and goddesses since ancient times. It can help you focus your psychic abilities, so it's great for spell work involving divination or any type of clairvoyance. Beech can also attract love, peace, and happiness or dial up the power of your spells. It also reduces stress, so it's perfect for protective amulets or talismans you want to carry with you during travels. A piece of beech wood will also help you keep your own energy private.

Oak: The oak is a powerful tree that helps you stay grounded during magic rituals and spell work. If you need to focus on something to straighten out karma, this is your tree. Its branches are used to make wands, and its leaves help call forth spirits and elemental energies. Oak is also good to use when cleansing your negative energy space. Oak is often carved and used as an altar tool during ceremonial magic. Its branches are also used to create magical tools, and its leaves were used for divination by the Celts.

Willow: Willow can be used to protect spells and stop evil spirits from harming you or your loved ones. It's also very helpful during magical protection if you want to direct the protection efforts of other trees or herbs. Willow is also widely used in healing magic, particularly in pain and discomfort. It can help relieve physical pain and provides relief from emotional pain. You can burn it in the same room as your altar or wear it to dispel bad luck.

White Oak Tree: This tree is sacred to magic rituals because of its associations with the Goddess energies. The ancient Egyptians also used it for various purposes, including treating eye problems, earaches, and headaches. White oak will help you raise your power so you can project your intentions outwards and bring about positive changes in the world around you.

Witch Hazel: The leaves and bark of this plant are used to create a magical force that is used in spells and rituals to attract love, abundance, and happiness. It's also good for protection magic, so if you're doing spell work around the house, put some in your ritual bath or wear it as an amulet to keep the forces of darkness away from you. Burn hazel on an incense burner to eliminate negative energy in your home or workspace. It's also good for meditation and for strengthening intuitive powers.

Rowan: To the Celts, the rowan tree represented rebirth, protection, and good fortune. It was also a sacred tree of the Norse. It can help you increase your connection with the spirits, so it's a fantastic herb or tree to burn during rituals or spells where you're trying to reach out to the other side. Rowan is often used in rituals to protect homes and ward off negativity. It's also used in money and health spells designed to improve digestion and relieve stomach issues.

Chapter 7: Hedge Divination

Divination involves being able to investigate the past and the future to get answers. Hedge witchcraft is a very adaptive practice, which means there are lots of divination techniques you could choose from. Let's look at each one in detail.

Tea Reading

Tea leaf reading is a common method of divination.
https://commons.wikimedia.org/wiki/File:Tea_leaf_reading.jpg

Since the dawn of time, people have been practicing divination. One of the most common methods is tea reading, also called tasseomancy. It's from a marriage of two words: Tassa, an Arabic word that translates to "cup," and Mancy, a Greek word that refers to divination itself.

European diviners during the medieval era would do all their readings by working with wax or lead splatters. However, tea soon became very popular, and so it naturally became a part of the divination process. You can choose to work with special cups for this process. Often, they'll have some magical symbols etched around the body or rim to help you with interpretation.

How to Read Tea Leaves

To read tea leaves, you'll have to brew a cup of tea, but unlike a regular cup, you're not going to strain out the leaves. Choose a teacup with a light color so it's easy for you to see what's happening at the bottom of the cup. When it comes to the tea you choose, you can work with any type you want. The only caveat is that they must be the loose-leaf kind. You want larger leaves because they're much easier for you to read. If you want to be specific about the kind of tea you choose, go for Earl Grey, as it has large, loose leaves. You could also work with Darjeeling. The Indian tea blends, while delicious, aren't the best for divination purposes because sometimes they have very fine particles, little twigs, and much smaller leaves.

When you or the seeker has finished drinking the tea, all you should have left in the cup are the leaves at the bottom of the cup. Give the cup a swirl three times, and then set the cup down and allow the contents to settle. The leaves will form a pattern which you can then interpret. You can work with symbols that are well known, having been handed down through generations. For instance, the leaves from an apple could mean education or knowledge. If it looks like a dog, it could mean "loyalty." A quick search on the Internet will show you the signs you can work with and their meanings. Keep in mind that just because you see a dog doesn't mean there's someone who is loyal. It could be a sign of the complete opposite. It all comes down to context and what your intuition is telling you.

Speaking of intuition, you can work with that instead of setting symbolic meanings. Just allow the leaves to speak to your spirit while you pass on the message to the querent. It's a good idea to get some practice with friends and family first so that you're sure you're on point more often than you aren't. Sit with the leaves, and as you look at them, pay attention to the feelings they drum up in you. Do you feel something positive or negative? What aspects of life are coming into your mind right now? Check in with the seeker to help you fine-tune the message from the leaves.

Keep in mind that sometimes you'll see more than one image. You could have a prominent image in the middle surrounded by smaller ones, or they could all be about the same size. Whatever you do, begin with the images from the cup's handle and then move around the cup in a clockwise manner. Are you working with a handle-less cup? Then start from the noon position (up north) and work your way clockwise around the cup.

Please make sure you keep notes as you read the leaves. Take pictures with your phone so you don't have to worry about accidentally upsetting the positions of the leaves. Pay attention to the first thing you notice because this is the most profound piece of information the divine is trying to communicate with you. Sometimes you may not get images but numbers or letters. You may also see ancient or alien symbols or even animal shapes.

Finally, divide the cup into different parts because placing the symbols or images is also important. The rim stands for matters that concern the here and now. The center is about the immediate future, which could be anywhere from seven days to a month. The bottom of the cup holds the key to your situation as a whole in the present.

Full Moon Scrying

Scrying is about looking into a reflective surface and allowing it to reveal the truth to you about the past, present, or future. It's commonly done with water, a crystal ball, or even a mirror. In the Egyptian Book of the Dead, you will find mentions of the process of scrying, especially regarding using Hathor's mirror to see what the future holds. The ancient Romans were no strangers to this, either. Before Christianity was introduced to the Celts, they would use crystals like beryl to learn about the future. Even the great Nostradamus practiced water scrying with candlelight to learn what he had to.

However, if you want to really draw more power into the process, working with the full moon is the way to go. The full moon represents intuition and has an aura of wisdom about it. We sense this deeply, which is why we feel so alive when the moon is at its fullest. This is because we have a connection with the lunar cycle.

You can do this indoors, but it's better outside because you're going to work with the reflection of the full moon's light on the water. It's best to work on the night of the full moon itself, but if you can't, you can do this on the night after or before. You'll need the sky to be clear.

How to Do Full Moon Scrying
You'll Need:
- A dark bowl
- A table or your altar
- A pitcher of water
- A journal and a pen

Steps:
1. Cast a circle by sprinkling salt on the floor around yourself and your altar. You should be barefoot.
2. Shut your eyes and pay attention to how you feel. Pay attention to the energy of the world around you as well. Become one with the sounds, smells, and feelings.
3. Now, turn your inner awareness to the moonlight. Feel its power flowing through you. Know and accept that you're connected to this power and therefore connected to the Universe.
4. When you feel ready, open your eyes and notice the night and its sights. You should be feeling very alert and grounded. This is the moon's power flowing through you.
5. Raise your pitcher and imagine that the water is full of the moon's wisdom as you pour it into the bowl. Imagine that the moonlight is charging the water even more with its energy. Fill the bowl, then set your pitcher down.
6. Stand over the bowl to keep your shadow from blocking the moonlight reflecting on the water.
7. Stare into the water. Don't strain to see images. Let them come on their own. You may see words or actual pictures or scenes on the water. Also, you may have ideas and concepts popping into your mind. Note everything you see and think down in a journal. You can stare into the water for a few minutes or hours.
8. If the messages don't make sense immediately, that's fine, and they could make more sense over the coming days. The message may pertain to you or to someone close to you.

9. Use the water to work more magic later, or water your plants with it.

Note that you can perform this scrying method with a lake or a river instead of a water bowl.

Pendulum Divination

Working with pendulums is one of the easiest ways to learn what you want from the divine. All you're doing is asking yes or no questions and then waiting for an answer. You can make your own pendulum or just buy an already made one. If you're going to make yours, you can work with any object that has weight. A stone or a crystal is great. You will also need a string or jeweler's wire and a light chain. Wrap the jeweler's wire around the stone and, at the top, create a loop. Put one end of your light chain through the loop. The chain must be long enough to allow you to swing the stone but not so long that you find it keeps bumping into things. Make sure you file off or tuck in the wire bits that stick out, so you don't hurt yourself.

When you've finished, it's time to charge your pendulum. Just put it in some salt water overnight. Please be sure that the stone you're working with can handle salt and water. Otherwise, you can just bury it underground overnight or let it absorb moonlight overnight.

After this, it's time to carry out calibration. Basically, you want to know what your pendulum does when it means yes and no. Hold on to the chain and let the stone hang, keeping your forearm balanced on a table for stability. Then ask an obvious yes or no question, such as, "Is my name Gary?" If it is, you should see it swing back and forth or side to side as *yes*. Ask another question that would yield you a no, then another that gives you a yes. Ask a couple more questions, and you should know what it means. Note that sometimes you may get circular movement instead, and other times your pendulum may not respond. When you've calibrated it, you can finally ask it whatever questions you want.

How to Use Your Pendulum for Divination

You will need to ask only yes or no questions, but you shouldn't let that make you feel limited because you can learn a lot from the right questions. You can work with a divination board, which has letters on it. It's almost like an Ouija board, as it has numbers and letters and words, maybe, no, and yes. You can also use your pendulum as a dowsing rod to help you find missing things. Move around the room you suspect the item is in and note if your pendulum moves faster (meaning you're close to it) or slower (meaning you're far from it). If you need to find something but only know the country or building, you can use a list of each state, a map, a list of each room, or the building's schematics. Let the pendulum hover over each place and pay attention to the one it seems most excited about as it moves. You could incorporate tarot cards if you want answers that require much more than a simple yes or no. Use the pendulum to lead you to the card, which you can then interpret as needed.

The Celtic Ogham

The word Ogham is from the name of the Celtic god Ogmios or Ogma. He's in charge of granting literacy and eloquence to one and all. The Ogham staves have letters of the Ogham alphabet and are used as divination tools for those who choose to practice their hedge craft the Celtic way. There were 20 letters in the Ogham alphabet; later, that number went up to 25. All the letters match up to a sound and represent a specific tree or wood. They also represent various aspects of what it means to be human.

If you want to, you can create your very own Ogham staves. All you need is to find twigs that are the same lengths or cut them into the same length. You'll need 26 of them, with the last one being the blank one. Ideally, each twig should be anywhere from 4 to 6 inches. Using sandpaper, smooth out the twigs and carve in the Ogham symbols on each, one symbol per twig. You can also paint them on if you prefer.

When you've finished, consider the meaning of each symbol. Sit with each one in meditation, soaking in their aura and unique interpretations. You should be able to feel the magic of each symbol. Make sure you're in the right headspace for this and that you will not be distracted. After this, consecrate the staves by asking your preferred deity for help, and then you can go ahead to work with the staves. To do this, keep them in a bag, then consider what you want to know. Stick your hand in the bag, give the staves a good shuffle, and then pull one out. The following is the Ogham alphabet and what each letter means:

Beth or Beith: Birch, new beginnings, rebirth, release, purification, change, hardiness, releasing of negative energies, learning of toxic habits, discovering toxic relationships, letting go of toxicity, a need to focus on the positive, time for emotional and spiritual regeneration, fruitfulness after hard times.

Luis: Rowan, blessings, protection, wisdom, insight, high awareness, intuition, trust, staying true to spiritual nature, staying grounded when unsure.

Fearn or Fern: Alder, the evolution of spirit, spring equinox, March, Bran, hardiness, perseverance, individuality, appreciation for others' uniqueness, mediation, instinct, wise counsel, the voice of reason.

Sallie or Suil: Willow, rapid growth, nourishment, April, healing, protection, moon cycles, female mysteries, female cycles, pain relief, flexibility, adaptability, openness to change, acceptance of unpleasant lessons for spiritual growth, the need to take a break, spiritual rest, trust in coming change, call for flexibility in spiritual matters.

Nionor Nin: Ash, the connection of the world within and the world without, creativity, sacrifice for higher goals, wisdom, consequences, spiritual interconnection, and the balance between the natural and supernatural.

Huath or Uathe: Hawthorn, defense, protection, cleansing, Beltane, fire, masculine energy, fertility, virility, the Fae, successful child conception, health, spiritual strength, overcoming problems, guidance, being a strength for others to draw on.

Duir or Dair: Oak, self-confidence, resilience, strength, domination, summer, doorways, success, money, fertility, good fortune, masculinity, durability, health, prevailing against difficulties, and unpredictability.

Tinne or Teine: Holly, evergreen, courage, immortality, home, hearth, stability, unity, protection, change, transition, blessing, a call to listen to intuition, quick response, adaptability to new situations, triumph, trust for instinct, the balance of logic and desire.

Coll or Call: Hazel, August, hazel moon, life force, creativity, wisdom, knowledge, divination, sacred waters, self-defense, using what you have, sharing what you know, seeking inspiration, allowing oneself to be led by the divine, working with art, receiving more inspiration.

Squirt or Ceirt: Apple tree, faithfulness, rebirth, love, magic, life's never-ending cycle, fertility, prosperity, the need to make the right choice, openness to new paths, receiving spiritual gifts, allowing things to not make sense.

Muin: Vines, wine, prophecy, truth, pausing before speaking, honesty, divination, moderation in life's pleasures.

Gort: Ivy, searching for yourself, wildness, growth, mysticism, evolution, spiritual development, Samhain, October, rebirth, death, life, good fortune for women, protection from magic, protection from curses, love, the banishment of all negative things and relationships, seeking answers from within, looking outside for spiritual allies.

Ng or nGeatal: Reed, purpose, action, health, healing, friends and family, leadership, rebuilding what's been torn down, bringing order back, proactivity over-reactivity, spiritual growth.

St or Straith or Straif: Blackthorn, control authority, triumph over enemies, strength, dark magic, the Morrigan, the Crone, expecting the unexpected, accepting change in plans, external influence, the start of a new journey, pleasant and unpleasant surprises to come.

Ruis: Elder, winter, endings, awareness from experience, maturity, rejuvenation, recovery, the Goddess, the Fae, preservation, transition, knowledge, maturity, a call to be childlike rather than childish, newness.

Ailim or Ailm: Elm, perspective, vision, Beltane, flexibility, the big picture, long-term goals, preparation, noting your progress, spiritual growth, wisdom, and others' inspiration and help.

Onn or Ohn: Gorse bush, long-term plans, determination, hope, perseverance, banishing the bad, manifesting desire, using your gifts to bless others, mentorship, leadership.

Ura or Uhr: Heather, generosity, passion, spiritual messengers, the Otherworld, assurance of victory, time to de-stress, physical, mental, and spiritual healing.

Eadhadh or Eadha: Courage, endurance, durability, success, strong will, triumph over enemies and stumbling blocks, protection, the Fae, bending but not breaking, adversity about to end, releasing of fear, allowing yourself to be vulnerable, focusing on your spiritual growth, taking the first step.

Iodhadh or Idad: Yew, Endings, death, new from the old, rebirth, major changes to come, time to release what doesn't serve, taking advantage of major transitions.

Eabhadh: Grove trees, conflict resolution, wise counsel, justice, spiritual harmony, clearing of misunderstandings, need for communication, leading by example, less talk, and more action, fairness, wisdom, and ethics.

Oi or Oir: Spindle, strength in vulnerability, family honor, fulfilling obligations, curiosity, connection to others.

Uillean: Honeysuckle, manifesting your desire, secret wants, goals, finding who you are, freedom to go after what you want, fulfilling dreams, enjoying life, holding on to values, uncovering mysteries.

Ifin or Iphin: Pine, vision, clear conscience, the need to stop feeling guilty, time to make amends, time to move on, being intellectual instead of emotional.

Amhancholl or Eamhancholl: Hazel, cleansing, purifying, releasing emotional baggage, releasing stale energies, reevaluating spiritual journey, rethinking priorities.

Chapter 8: Kitchen Magic

Hedge witches have been around for centuries and have learned the magic of using their cooking skills in many ways. What hedge witches typically practice is known as kitchen magic. Kitchen magic can be practiced by anyone interested in it, regardless of their spirituality or belief system. Whether you are looking to make new friends while feeding your community or joining a coven that shares your pagan beliefs, this chapter will help you get started on practicing kitchen magic as an everyday hedge witch.

Kitchen Magic is fun and powerful. It all starts from the hearth, which is where the entire home is fueled from. It's a practice that is very ancient, practiced by females who were well aware of the power of plants and herbs and who knew how to channel that power to achieve different effects, from healing and blessing to protection from the evil eye.

A kitchen is a place in the home with many superstitions and stories. Originally, the hearth was fashioned to make offerings to the divine and partake of these offerings. Where others only see ingredients for cooking, the kitchen witch can see and feel the magic waiting to be put to good use. You could think of the process of kitchen magic as being like meditation, where everything that's done in the kitchen, from cooking to cleaning, is imbued with magical intention.

Like several other types of magic, kitchen magic can be used for good or bad purposes. The recipes you will find in this chapter are examples of good kitchen magic. You can transform your kitchen into a place of alchemy, where you are the magician who can mix ingredients to produce magic results and create wonderful dishes that delight the senses and have numerous magical properties.

Your kitchen magic doesn't have to be limited to food. You can use your cooking skills and knowledge of kitchen magic to create some amazing candles and other paraphernalia. Try mixing all-natural ingredients, like beeswax, soy wax, and essential oils to make scented candles. There are hundreds of different recipes for making these natural candles online. You can also use kitchen magic for more practical purposes by making your own laundry detergent or cleaning products.

No one's a better hostess than the hedge witch who works kitchen magic. You can trust that everything in her kitchen is a magical tool. She can wield her steak knife as a boline or an athame. She can use a carrot as a wand. It doesn't matter what she works with. What matters is the attitude she pursues her craft with, so if you want to practice, you should consider your home a sacred space.

What Kitchen Witches Do

A kitchen witch can grow her own herbs if she wants to. She can work with them to help bless others or perform a much-needed cleansing. She can also practice tasseomancy to help her guests, whip up a special brew of tea to help you if you've got a nasty cold or a case of the blues, and much more. As a hedge witch, you're also a kitchen witch if you choose to work magic with your food. You don't need to subscribe to a certain faith or let your religious leanings keep you away from your craft, either. You'll know if you have a penchant for kitchen magic based on how you approach cooking. If you have a passion for whipping up good meals and love when others enjoy your cooking, you're not too far away from becoming a kitchen witch yourself. All you need is some magical intent.

So, You Think You're a Kitchen Witch, Too?

A kitchen witch is also called a *cottage witch*; her spells are her magical meals. You can work with deities or spirits as you cook to draw on their energy and make your spells even more powerful. If you find that you're drawn to kitchen magic but don't know where to begin, the first thing you should do is keep things simple. This form of magic is very practical and to the point. What's going to change in how you cook is you will bring more mindfulness and intention to every part of the process. Because you do this, you're also going to notice that the way you think of your home and personal space will also change.

Your countertop and stove will both serve as your altar, so you can put the spiritual items that remind you of what you want to achieve with your magic onto them. Also, you want to set up your home so that when people come in, they feel relaxed, like they're escaping the world's harsh realities.

You may want to take up some gardening, as it's a great thing to have fresh herbs on hand for whatever meal you want to prepare. All you need is a window ledge with enough sunlight to grow your herbs. As a bonus, growing plants in your home brings lovely, magical energy. If you can't grow herbs or aren't interested, that's fine too. You can work with dry options; just because they're dry doesn't mean they've lost their potency.

According to traditions and lore, you should also do your homework on what each herb and plant you're working with represents. Check out the significance of each kitchen tool and action as well. For instance, when sweeping dirt off your floor, you should empty it outside the home to allow more good fortune into your space and your life. So, the next time you do this, being more mindful of the spiritual implication guarantees you will draw in good fortune.

Setting Up the Space

Your altar shouldn't have clutter on it, so take care if that's the case. Use your hands or a magic broom to sweep away all stale, stuck, negative energies still hovering around the space when it's all gone. On your altar, put some statues or symbols that represent the energies and beings you want to work your craft with. You can have general ones or specific ones for particular spells you want to cast.

You should also place the tools you'll often use on your altar, like utensils, spoons, chopsticks, your pestle and mortar, knives, athame, wand, and so on. You'll also need to have your grimoire handy, so you can refer to the spells you've got in them or make notes as needed about what you're doing differently with the spell you're working on. You can also place your sacred herbs and other foods here. Let's not forget you'll need your cauldron. You don't have to use it, though, as it could just be symbolic. You get to figure out what's the best option for you.

Working with Deities

You don't have to devote yourself to one deity over another. You can work with several to make different spells. For instance, if you want to make a lucky meal, working with Fortuna is a good idea. She is the goddess of all fortune. Another goddess you can work with is Annapurna, who oversees food and nourishment according to the Hindus. Anna means "food," and *Purna* means full or complete. She makes sure that we have sustenance. According to lore, her consort, Shiva, once declared that males were the superior gender. So, Annapurna disappeared in her anger and, as a result, the world was plunged into a terrible famine. Everyone was saved only when she decided to return and share her bounty with the world. Working with her will bless your spells.

You could also work with Andhrimnir. He is the Aesir Gods' chef. Lore has it that each day, he heads out to slaughter Saehrimnir the boar, and then he cooks it to offer to the Gods. Each night, Saehrimnir comes back to life. Andhrimnir is good to work with because he is an amazing cook, and so if you want to do better and give your loved ones a meal they won't forget in a hurry, work with him.

Hestia, the Greek goddess of the hearth, is another deity who can help you. She's all about family, warmth, love, and food. According to lore, Hestia was the one Zeus trusted to make sure the Olympus fire wouldn't burn out. She did this by offering fatty meat to be burned as a sacrifice. Work with her, and you'll have meals that strengthen the connection between everyone under your roof or taking part in eating the meal.

Crafting Magical Spells

While every ingredient in the meal is magical by virtue of you acknowledging that, the key knowledge you need to understand surrounds the spices and herbs and their energy properties. When you understand their powers, you can simply add the relevant herb to your meal to make it magical. Here's a quick list of the basic spices and herbs you will be working with and what they bring to the table, magically speaking:

- **Rosemary:** Good for improving memory, encouraging clear thought, protection, and boosting strength and courage. Also, good for blessing.

- **Allspice**: Excellent for energy, happiness, peace, and success.

- **Cinnamon:** Increases psychic powers, gives success, and promotes healing.

- **Ginger:** Acts as an energy enhancer and accelerates the speed of your spell's manifestation. Also, good for power, money, and love spells.

- **Coriander:** Use this for money and health matters.
- **Cloves:** Used for purification, protection, and success.
- **Basil:** Boosts creativity, inspires courage, and is great for protection. Also brings you abundance, good luck, psychic power, lust, and love.
- **Bay leaves:** Wisdom, divination, prosperity, protection, love, and joy.
- **Garlic:** Excellent for protection from negative energies. Also, good for attaining power.
- **Parsley:** Add this to your spells for purification.
- **Mint:** Use to draw in success, love, money, and lust. Encourages happiness, peace, and safety.

Mint encourages happiness.
Commonists, CC BY-SA 4.0 <https://creativecommons.org/licenses/by-sa/4.0>, via Wikimedia Commons: https://commons.wikimedia.org/wiki/File:Mint_leaves_(Mentha_spicata).jpg

- **Nutmeg:** Use this for intuition and psychic growth. Also, use it to encourage peace, happiness, and prosperity.
- **Sage:** For spiritual wisdom, divination, protection, purification, longevity, courage, wealth, and prosperity in all your affairs.

Kitchen Magic Recipes

You'll use several ingredients with different magical properties when you cook a meal. The trick here, therefore, is to focus your attention and energy on manifesting the properties of the specific ingredients you want to use. Some people have recipes like "Bye Bad Luck Pie" or "Feel Better Veggie Soup," but the truth is that the same pie or soup can be used for other purposes than warding off bad luck or making someone feel better because there are other ingredients in them.

So, think about your intention for your spell, then consider the herbs and spices that would create that energy, and then prepare the meal focusing on those energies as you work with those herbs. It's impractical to name one recipe after a specific purpose. What will you do, make a cinnamon pie with cinnamon as the only ingredient? It makes no sense. So keep your intention in mind as you cook, and when it's time to add the ingredients whose energies you seek to use, say a quick prayer stating what you want it to help you with before adding it to your meal. So, let's get into some recipes you can try out!

Chicken Marbella

Thanks to Tasty.co for this recipe.

You'll Need:

- 3 lbs. chicken (protects your family and home)
- 1 head garlic, puréed or grated (offers protection)
- ¾ cup dried apricot (love)
- 3 tablespoons dried oregano (love, luck, protection)
- 2 teaspoons kosher salt (purifies and protects)
- ⅓ cup olive oil (fosters protection, peace, and loyalty)
- 3 red plums, pitted, quartered (encourages relaxation, love, and lust)
- 1 cup green olives (same as olive oil)
- ⅓ cup red wine vinegar (joy, health, physical strength)
- 6 cups couscous (nourishment, abundance)
- ⅓ cup dry rosé wine (joy, friendship)

- ½ cup brined capers (offers protection and love)
- ⅓ cup fresh basil, sliced thin (fosters prosperity and love)
- ⅔ cup light brown sugar (for improving mood, making people favor you, fostering love)
- 3 dried bay leaves (offers psychic protection)

Note that you can use a bubbly rosé wine instead of dry rosé wine. You can also use Himalayan pink salt instead of kosher salt.

Steps:

1. Use the salt to season the chicken evenly.
2. Rub 1 tablespoon of oregano and the garlic all over and into the chicken.
3. Using a glass baking dish about 9 x 13 inches, mix your olive oil, green olives, red wine vinegar, 2 tablespoons of oregano, capers, apricots, plums, and bay leaves.
4. Add the chicken to the dish and turn it in it to coat it with the mix. Let the skin side face upward.
5. With plastic wrap, cover the dish. Let the chicken sit in the fridge for 12 hours or overnight.
6. Preheat your oven to 375 degrees Fahrenheit.
7. Take the chicken out of the fridge. Give it half an hour to return to room temperature.
8. Pat the chicken dry with a paper towel.
9. Sprinkle the brown sugar onto the chicken skin.
10. Pour the rose around the chicken, but not onto the skin.
11. Bake for 35 to 40 minutes, or until your thermometer reads 160 degrees Fahrenheit when you insert it into the fold of a thigh close to the bone. The skin should be a nice, golden brown at this point.
12. Take the chicken out of the oven and let it cool for ten minutes. The temperature will go up by 5 degrees, thanks to the residual heat.
13. Serve the chicken with the sauce along with couscous. Use basil for garnishing.

Herbal Chicken Roast

You'll Need:
- 1 whole chicken (cleaned)
- 1 onion, cut into chunky bits (for getting rid of illness)
- ½ stick of salted butter (provides nourishment in any aspect of life)
- 1 handful of fresh herbs (combine lemon balm, thyme, and rosemary)
- 2 lemons, unpeeled, cut into chunks (for purification)
- Salt to taste (for protection and purification)
- Pepper to taste (also for protection and purification)

Steps:
1. Preheat your oven to 350 degrees Fahrenheit.
2. Clean your chicken if it's not already clean. Get rid of the innards, wash the whole thing with water, then pat it dry with paper towels to remove unnecessary moisture.
3. Squeeze one of the lemon chunks into the chicken's middle, then stuff the chicken with your onions, fresh herb, and the other lemon chunk. Use a string to tie the chicken's legs together, securing all the stuffing.
4. Put the chicken on a platter and let it bake for 20 minutes for every pound it weighs at 350 degrees Fahrenheit.
5. When there are only 40 minutes of baking left, or just before the skin gets crisp, melt your butter. Pour the melted butter over the chicken and slide it back into the oven.
6. Every ten to fifteen minutes, use the juices in the pan to baste the chicken.
7. Take it out and wait for it to cool before you serve.

What other recipes do you already know? Consider their spices, herbs, and other ingredients. How can you make them into magical spells? There are no limits, and there's no wrong way to do this.

Chapter 9: Sacred Sabbats and Rituals

Hedge witches are in tune with nature, which means they are aware of its changes throughout the year. In this chapter, we will look at each of the eight festivals on the Wheel of the Year, focusing on the pagan aspects of the cycle.

Sabbats

Sabbats are holidays, and they are observed to mark the beginning of each season and their halfway points. They are spread out evenly all through the year. These Sabbats are rooted in Germanic and Celtic paganism. The word Sabbat is etymologically from the Hebrew language and is a central concept in Judaism. It's connected to the word "Sabbath," a time to gather to ensure certain rites and rituals are carried out.

The Eight Pagan Holidays or Sabbats

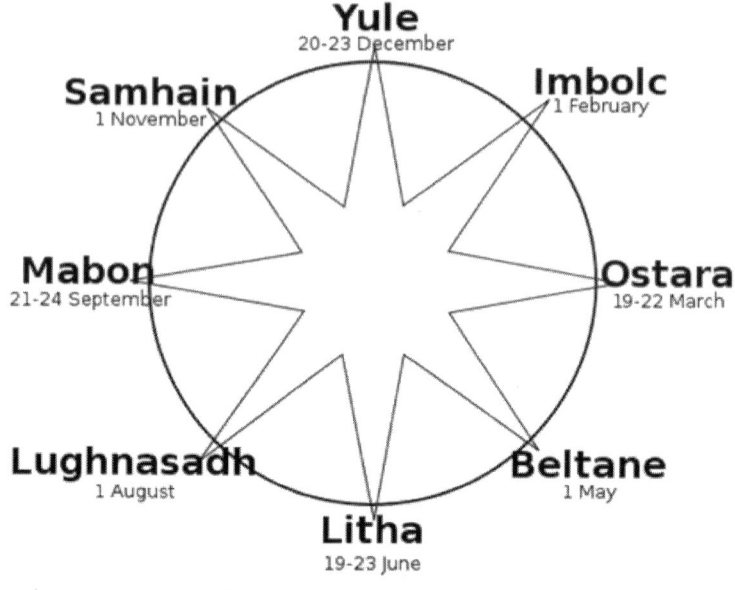

Yule — 20-23 December
Imbolc — 1 February
Ostara — 19-22 March
Beltane — 1 May
Litha — 19-23 June
Lughnasadh — 1 August
Mabon — 21-24 September
Samhain — 1 November

The eight pagan holidays calendar.
https://commons.wikimedia.org/wiki/File:Wheel_of_the_Year.svg

Yule: This is the Winter Solstice, which happens from December 20 to 23. At this point, you'll notice there are shorter days than usual. This is when everyone does what they must to be ready for the cold times to come. It's a good time to remember that the element of fire and the sun brings warmth to one and all, and they both make life possible on this planet. This is when people commonly decorate trees with food, specifically the kind of food that does well in cold times. This is meant to remind one and all that even when things get too dark and cold, growth is an ongoing process, and life will never end.

Christmas has certain traditions that it borrowed from this Sabbat. For instance, there's the yule log, originally intended to keep negative spirits from the Otherworld or around you and bless you with excellent luck. Then there's the mistletoe, which was used for the same purpose. Yule is a very old tradition, one of the oldest as far as human civilization is concerned. The winter solstice is marked on the year's shortest day.

How to Celebrate Yule

1. Yule is an excellent time to get together with your family and friends.

2. You could choose to light your Yule log, and you don't have to cut down a tree to do this.
3. Decorate your home with red and white.
4. Bring in the Yule energy with a gift for someone you love.
5. Wear a red ribbon as it symbolizes love and passion, but more importantly, it symbolizes love's eternal endurance through strife and trials.
6. Light candles and decorate with mistletoe, holly, ivy, yew, or pine boughs.
7. Hang baubles on the tree or around your home or spirit house to bring good luck in abundance all year round. You could also hang wind chimes which will quickly bring you into harmony with the moving energies of spirit as they sing their tune throughout your dwelling.

Imbolc: This falls on February 2 and is held in honor of the goddess Brigid, who blesses one and all with fertility. In other words, it's like a violent spring. This Sabbat is when you gather with others and celebrate the coming of spring, spring itself, and other good things in your life. It's also a time when we assess our personal lives to see if some improvement needs to be made to how we live our lives. It's when you set out candles, buns, and other foods and decorate them in honor of the coming of spring. It should remind one and all that the hard times are almost over.

Imbolc is also a sacred time to meditate on love which is meant to lead to happiness, peace, recognition from others around you, and a general sense of well-being. This reminds one and all that for something to truly be considered sacred, it must be about more than just your own life; it must also be about the well-being of others. For this reason, it was important in ancient times to do something that would benefit everyone living around you and yourself.

This is the midpoint between the winter solstice and spring equinox. During this time, you'll notice that the days are getting longer. That means it's time to enjoy lighter foods and, in general, more optimism in general. The fire element at work here is flame or light/heat, while water remains the element of purification. We do everything we can during this time to ensure a good growing season, so we can grow our food and create wealth for ourselves and our families. The best way to do that is to ensure the past year's leftover and bad energy or spirits don't stick around but rather move on. We do that by sweeping our homes and businesses clean using reed brooms. The old furniture is removed, and new, fresh furniture is brought in. We also have the tradition of lighting a candle on the windowsill during this time to signal that spring has arrived and life will continue onward. This holiday isn't entirely about fertility as many people think. It's about celebrating the abundance it brings in general.

How to Celebrate Imbolc

1. You could make a feast in honor of Brigid and all the blessings she has brought to your life and to all those around you. Have a good time and eat, drink, and be merry!
2. Light a candle on the windowsill to signal new growth and the future ahead of you.
3. Celebrate the arrival of spring by decorating with flowers, plants, wheat sheaves, or new growth in general. For example, if it's February 2, you could decorate fresh-cut spruce branches sprinkled with winter salt (see description below). This is meant to signify renewal and a clean slate for you after the harsh winter months.
4. You could also decorate the house with flowers or wheat stalks.
5. Make wheat saffron buns, which will remind you of the importance of food in your life and represent an ancient form of this holiday.
6. Make sure your home is clean, as well as your spirit house or temple if you have one in your home. Then you'll know that the bad spirits that may have been lingering around since the past year are now gone and won't be coming back anytime soon. And if they do, at least you'll know it was because they were invited.
7. Create a wish and make it known to the goddess, then get back to living the rest of your life knowing that Brigid has taken your wish into account, but it is up to you to make the most of whatever happens.

Ostara: This is the Spring Equinox, and it falls between March 19 and 22. That means that at this time it's sunny and warm. It's also a day for renewal and renewal of the natural state of things. This is when you do what is necessary to ensure your life goes well, both personally and professionally. We're talking about ensuring there's nothing negative in your life that needs to be removed, as well as making sure everything you added over the winter has a chance to bloom. This is also a time for romantic love, fidelity in marriage, one-on-one friendship relationships, membership in a group or society, and work partnerships. You'll notice you're more interested in sex and romance than in religion, which is also a sign of spring.

The elements of water and spirit merge at this time, which means it is time to make peace with existing conditions and with the past. You'll invite others up to your home for food and conversation, which is meant to give each other strength. Because it's the Spring Equinox, this is also the best time of year to plant new seeds or plants if you can add some beauty to your home. It's also when we move from our homes into our new homes and into acquiring new careers. The Christian holiday Easter borrows heavily from this feast and is actually in honor of the goddess Eostre, who is of Germanic origin.

How to Celebrate Ostara

1. You could decorate with flowers and plants, especially seeds and saplings, if you have them.
2. You could also create traditional Easter baskets filled with foods such as eggs, bread, and wine.
3. You can also decorate to celebrate love, oaths of fidelity, loyalty, and friendship by bringing in a bouquet of flowers for your porch or front door or by putting up a new broom in your home if you haven't had one for many months.
4. You can also wait until April 1 to work on all future vows of fidelity, friendship, and romantic love during Ostara.
5. You can make sure you decorate your home with flowers, plants, wheat sheaves, or even indoor plants to signify the renewal of life.
6. Try to find a new job, whether that's in your current career or an entirely different one, to ensure you're getting ahead in life and allow the flow of Ostara's fertile energy. Make sure you live up to your vows of fidelity.
7. Take walks in the woods and nature to help cleanse your spirit and make peace with the past and the current natural world around you.

Beltane: This is celebrated on Mayday, which is May 1. It's also called the Festival of Fire and marks the time between the spring equinox and the coming summer solstice. At this point, spring has made progress, and it's starting to give way to more warmth and longer days that mark summer. The etymological root of Beltane is from Bel, a Celtic god, and *teine,* a Gaelic word that translates to "fire." At this time, you're expected to show your appreciation for spring, thankful that it makes all things fertile physically and in other aspects of your life. At this time, people dance around the maypole, often with crowns of flowers on their heads. It's also believed that the veil between the physical world and the Otherworld is thin at this time, and therefore it's a good idea to perform magic that requires extra power. It's also a time to celebrate the coming harvest.

How to Celebrate Beltane

1. You could also decorate your home to honor the coming summer using plants such as wheat sheaves, wheat stalks, corn stalks, and even fresh-picked holly twigs.
2. Honor the god Bel by offering him grains on your altar.
3. Celebrate the coming harvest by placing three glasses of beer or ale in a triangle shape around your home for the following three days.
4. Celebrate the birth of love, friendship, and devotion to your favorite deity or goddess at this time.
5. Make sure you dance around the maypole with your friends and have lots of joy, laughter, and fun.
6. You can also clean your home by removing unnecessary things.
7. You can plant seeds and saplings to honor fertility and new growth, as well as to honor life.

Litha: This is marked between June 19 and 23. It's also known as the summer solstice or midsummer, and unlike Yule, it is the day of the year with the longest day and the shortest night. You can do the work you must at this time, but you should also celebrate as you now have long days that will allow enough time to achieve goals and be merry. This is when many will get engaged, and it's also when blessings are pronounced over the land, so the harvest will be bountiful indeed. Traditionally, this time is celebrated with torchlight processions through the land and bonfires. These are meant to remind one and all of the power and glory of the sun, which will eventually lose its power over time as summer gives way to winter once more.

How to Celebrate Litha

1. You can decorate your home with plants and flowers such as roses, honeysuckle, and foxglove.

2. This is a time to catch up on any summer goals.
3. You can honor the deities of fertility and the sun with your home decoration or by placing their statues or pictures around the place.
4. You can celebrate the coming of love, friendship, and romance with those you love.
5. Make offerings to the deities by throwing food onto bonfires, although not just any food, but fruit and nuts such as chestnuts and walnuts, as well as milk or milk products such as butter and cream, to honor these gods.
6. Take lots of walks outside to enjoy the summer air and to help cleanse your mind of everything you've been thinking about for so long.
7. Plant new seeds and saplings to honor fertility and prosperity.

Lughnasadh: This is also called the first harvest, and it's marked on August 1. It's a time between summer and autumn when the very first harvests are brought in from the fields. It's about celebrating that the earth worked with the sun to yield more than enough fruit and grain for one and all. It's important to give thanks for the good that we receive. This is such a joyful time that many also choose this holiday to get married. The Sabbat is named after Lugh, the light god. It is said that Tailtiu, his mother, helped to prepare Ireland's lands so that crops could be planted successfully.

How to Celebrate Lughnasadh

1. You can decorate your home with plants such as wheat sheaves, wheat stalks, corn stalks, and even fresh-picked holly twigs.
2. You can also decorate your home with pumpkins and painted eggs to celebrate the year's first harvests.
3. At this time, many will make large bonfires where food is traditionally cooked in large cauldrons to allow the flames to impart good luck and blessings of prosperity to the land. This is because Lughnasadh is a time when fire is believed to be very powerful and magical.
4. Make offerings to the sun god and goddess by throwing food onto bonfires.
5. Celebrate your mother or father that evening with a feast, especially since you're celebrating their harvest.

6. You can also pray for power over the year and abundance in all you do by holding a ritual around the fire to help balance the energies of your home to help you all be prosperous throughout all aspects of life (work, love, and play).
7. Wear new clothes that signify fertility and abundance at this time, if possible, as well as new shoes if footwear is necessary to do what must be done during this time.

Mabon: This is also known as the autumn equinox, which holds from September 21 to 24. It's when autumn comes, marking the time for the harvest to be reaped. It's a time of plenty, and all the labor that people have put into their projects comes to fruition at this time so that preparations can be made for the cold months to come.

How to Celebrate Mabon

1. You can decorate your altar with fresh fruit such as apples and pears.
2. You can also hang dried fruit such as raisins and cranberries around your home to signify the abundance of good fruit harvested at harvest time.
3. You can make paper mâché masks that look like pumpkins and scarecrows made out of straw to honor the coming of fall and its harvesting seasons.
4. Try to help friends and family who are struggling during this time by giving them support and prayers.
5. You can celebrate the coming of love, friendship, and prosperity by giving thanks to your favorite deity at this time as well.
6. Clean your home by getting rid of unnecessary things.
7. Wear jewelry made of silver or moonstones, which are believed to celebrate the god of the earth at this time, and give thanks for what you have received.

Samhain: This is also known as Halloween and is celebrated either on October 31 or November 1. It's a magical time of the year, being the only other time the veil between our world and the Otherworld is thin, letting the living and dead interact and draw on each other's power as needed. It's also called All Hallow's Eve, the time for one and all to pay their respects to familiars, family, and other loved ones who have passed. To celebrate this time, it is customary to have Jack Lanterns made from pumpkins to light a pathway for those who have passed on, so they can find their way to their next adventure. You can use this time to seek guidance, get rid of stubbornly lingering negativity, seek help with difficult or confusing situations, and begin the new year on the right footing for a higher chance you'll end it successfully.

How to Celebrate Samhain

1. You can decorate your home with fresh fruit as well as pumpkins, candles, and Jack O'Lanterns.
2. You can also make a special meal, such as a feast, around the table where you and your loved ones are seated.
3. Set intentions for the New Year, saying what you will do and want to achieve.
4. Bury and burn old things that have no meaning or power to allow for new things to affect your life. This includes burning candles as offerings as well.
5. Make sure you use this Sabbat's energy to eliminate any bad habits.
6. You can also reset the energies of your home by burning sage or ridding yourself of clutter and unwanted items that may take up space inside your home.
7. Wear dark colors at this time so that you can make contact with the dead and seek guidance on how to accomplish what you wish to do in your life.

Chapter 10: Your Hedge Spell Book

People often wonder when the best time is to practice spells. It doesn't matter if you do it in the morning, noon, or at night. You could have "set times" and still not get results because you're not in the right frame of mind or your intentions aren't clear. In other words, the only thing that matters with a spell is you know exactly what you want it to accomplish, and you're in a state of mind that is completely focused, free from distractions and worries.

To borrow from the psychedelic community, you could say effective spells are less about time and more about "set and setting," with the *set* being your frame of mind before, during, and after the spell, and the *setting* being your location. You should perform the spell somewhere you won't be disturbed. Make it somewhere that feels right to you, so you can focus on the task at hand and not lose energy trying to make an unfamiliar or uncomfortable space comfortable.

A final note: While specific herbs are mentioned in each spell, please note there's no rule that says you must work with them. For instance, if an abundance spell calls for High John the Conqueror, but you don't have that on hand, feel free to replace that with another spice or herbs like mint or bay leaf.

Magic Money Spell

This spell involves creating a money bag that will draw prosperity to you or whoever you perform it for. Please be certain that you're ready for the money to come and will be responsible with it, because it works like, well, like a charm.

You'll Need:

- Allspice (1 pinch)
- Some drops of bergamot essential oil
- A black marker
- A paper bag
- Play money of different denominations

Steps:

1. Use your marker to draw any currency signs you want on it. Make sure they're prominent. More is better.
2. Put the play money into the bag.
3. Add in your allspice and bergamot oil.
4. Squeeze the top of the bag closed and give the bag a shake. You want the herbs to be all over every bill in the bag. As you shake it, affirm that money comes to you quickly and easily.
5. When you've finished, move around your space, putting the paper bills in different spots where no one will move them.
6. When you've finished, carefully fold the paper baggie, and keep it somewhere safe. Expect that money will begin flowing to you from unexpected sources.

Wallet Charging Spell

If you feel like money hasn't really been flowing lately, it could be because the energy of abundance and flow is being blocked by your inability or refusal to be on the lookout for it. Fortunately, there's a way to get things flowing again, and the wallet charging spell is a very potent one that will bring you as much financial relief as you require.

check (you can use an actual check or print one off the internet)
- Your wallet or purse
- 1 teaspoon of dill

Steps:
1. First, figure out how much money you need to get by each month and still have enough to spare.
2. Next, fill in the check to yourself with that amount.
3. Fold the check-in half and put the dill in the crease.
4. Fold the check with the dill as tight as possible to seal in the herb.
5. Put this folded check in your wallet. It will draw money to you

Plentiful Pockets Charm

People don't understand about being abundant and prosperous because money and wealth can come from sources other than the usual or expected. Being open-minded to the flow of abundance like this puts you in a position to receive more of the universe's bounty. The plentiful pockets charm is a good one to help you open your eyes to the opportunities to make wealth that are all around you.

You'll Need:
- A string or some twine
- A square piece of green flannel (at least 4 inches on each side)
- 1 Piece of High John the Conqueror root (draws abundance)
- 1 Teaspoon chamomile (dried)

Steps:
1. Set the flannel on your altar.
2. On the flannel, place the High John the Conqueror root and the chamomile.
3. Use the flannel to create a pouch of sorts by pulling the corners together. As you do this, say, or concentrate on your intention to receive money and wealth that blesses one and all.

4. Use the twine or string to tie the pouch securely. Take this around with you to use it to attract money-making opportunities and financial blessings that are nothing short of amazing to you.

Blossoming Money

This spell calls for apples, which represent the energy of harvest, prosperity, and bounty. You can do this spell whenever you want, but if you perform this when the moon waxes, you will have an explosive inflow of money or money-making opportunities.

You'll Need:

- Apple blossoms (dried)
- New pennies
- A lidded glass jar

Steps:

1. Put all the apple blossoms and pennies you can into the jar. Make sure you mix them up instead of putting them in layers.
2. Cover the jar and hold it in both hands as you set an intention or say a prayer that your finances will continue to prosper.
3. Take this jar to your yard and find a nice spot where it can't be unearthed to bury.
4. Got an apple tree? You can bury your jar beneath that instead of any random spot to take advantage of the tree's energy to boost your spell.

Love by Candlelight Spell

If you're ready for love after having been on your own for far too long, this is a wonderful spell to use to get you open to the possibility of receiving love and drawing your perfect match your way.

You'll Need:

- 1 pink candle
- Dried, powdered dill
- Almond or grape seed or jojoba oil

Steps:
1. Use a sharp object to carve a heart into the side of the candle or carve the word, Love. If you want, you can do both and add other symbols representing the idea of being loved. As you carve, chant, or sing the word "love," let it fill your heart.
2. When you've finished carving, rub some oil on your candle.
3. Take your candle and dress it with the dill. Let it be completely dressed.
4. Light your candle and set it down. Bring your gaze to the flame and feel its energy entering and enveloping you inside.
5. Now, imagine that you are full of loving energy. You can imagine it as a beautiful, soft pink light. See and feel it as it radiates outside you, filling the whole room and then the whole world. Realize that you deserve to love and be loved as you want. Affirm that you're worthy of love in its fullest, truest form.
6. Now, imagine being embraced by a lover. Feel what it's like to have their skin on yours. Allow yourself to smile and notice the warmth in your chest.
7. Let the candle burn until it goes out on its own, and then bury it outside close to your home.

Heart "Unbreaker" Spell

It's not easy to deal with breakups and betrayals in love. It's often hard to mend what's broken. With this spell, though, you will be able to heal much faster and better than you ever thought possible while integrating the lessons you learned from your relationship. As this is a spell meant to rid yourself of something, you can take advantage of the waning moon phase. However, if you can't wait till then, feel free to do it when you need to.

You'll Need:
- A bonfire or a fireplace
- Flammable items connected to whoever broke your heart
- Witch hazel branches (dried)
- Stinging nettle branches (dried)
- 1 Pinch of ginger (dried, powdered)
- A paper bag

Steps:

1. Take all the things that belong to your ex-lover and put them into the bag.
2. Put the witch hazel and stinging nettle into the bag.
3. Fold the top of the bag shut, and then fold the bag itself as small as you can, so it's not bigger than a packet.
4. Get your fire ready. When it's blazing hot, put the packet into the flame, aiming so that it lands right in the middle. Then, as it burns, repeat, "I intend to release this person." Intend that they no longer have power over you and that all the bonds keeping you together are hereby dissolved for eternity; if you feel the need to cry, allow the tears to flow and draw on their energy to empower your spell.
5. Toss the dried ginger in, intending that it boosts the speed at which your heart recovers.
6. When the packet and its contents are completely burned, let the fire die out naturally, and wait for everything to cool down.
7. Take the cool ashes out and take them as far from your home or ritual space as possible. Throw them out somewhere with a lot of wind to carry them away so that you no longer feel bad about things ending.

Love in the Pocket Charm

High John the Conqueror root is also very useful for fertility and sexual magnetism. You'll find that working with it allows you to be very confident in your sexuality, attracting love and suitable partners.

You'll Need:

- Red thread
- High John the Conqueror root
- 1 Red candle

Steps:

1. Carve the word "love" and the shape of a heart into the side of your red candle.
2. Light the candle.
3. While it burns, hold the High John the Conqueror root in both hands, and in your mind's eye, imagine your hands imbuing it with

the power of love and raw attraction.
4. Take the red thread and tie it around the root, intending that lovers will be drawn to you.
5. Keep this in your pocket and watch the magic happen.

Pocket Protection Charm

It's a good idea to always have something to keep you safe no matter where you go, and so there's no better charm than one designed to do just that and can fit into your pocket.

You'll Need:
- Red yarn or string
- A square of red fabric (3 inches on all sides)
- Amethyst (just one small piece)
- ½ Teaspoon rosemary (dried)
- ½ Teaspoon peppermint (dried)

Steps:
1. Set your red fabric on your altar.
2. Put the herbs and the crystal in the middle of the fabric.
3. Hold the fabric by the corners and pull it up to form a little pouch.
4. Use the red yarn to secure the fabric into a pouch. As you do so, intend to always be safe and always protected.
5. You can wear this around your neck or carry it in your pocket wherever you go.

Basil Protection Bag

Basil is amazing for staying safe from bad energy, deliberate magical attacks, curses, and bad luck. All you need to do is use it in your bath each day.

You'll Need:
- Fresh basil (you can use dry basil if that's not available)
- A cheesecloth bag with a drawstring

Steps:
1. Fill the bag with fresh basil
2. Run a bath. Make it a warm one. Let the bag hang from the faucet to let the water run through it.
3. Take a bath as usual.
4. When you're ready to come out, intend that all things negative have left your body, mind, and spirit, then come out.
5. Take the bag outside your home and bury it far away.

Mugwort Deep Sleep Spell

This is a good spell for when you're stressed out by the events of the day and you would like to sleep but are having trouble because you're anxious.

You'll Need:
- 1 teaspoon honey
- 1 cup of hot water
- 1 mug
- 1 teaspoon mugwort (dried)

Steps:
1. Put the mugwort into your mug.
2. Pour in hot water and let the mugwort steep for 15 minutes.
3. With a strainer, separate the tea from the plant matter.
4. Add honey if you want.
5. Before drinking it, make up your mind that you'll have a good night's sleep and pleasant dreams too. Then drink your tea.

Mugwort tea is not recommended for those who are nursing or pregnant.

Menstrual Pain Relief Spell

For some women, menstrual cycles can be incredibly frustrating. They have to deal with mood switches, irritability, anxiety, loads of pain, restlessness, and so on. This is an excellent spell if you know that your periods tend to be very problematic. You can work to make sure that you feel better.

You'll Need:
- 1 tablespoon rue
- Garnet
- Carnelian
- Moonstone
- 1 White candle
- 1 Red drawstring bag (small)

Steps:
1. Light your candle.
2. Spend five minutes looking into the flame.
3. As you look into the flame, imagine that your body is healing in your mind's eye. Imagine that a white light moves through your body, removing all the pain and making you feel more comfortable as it leaves with the bleeding.
4. Put the rue into the drawstring pouch while you say a little prayer or affirmation, intending that you will not be defeated or made to feel low by your cycle. Affirm that you are powerful, strong, and healthy and that all discomfort leaves your body now.
5. Close the bag by pulling the drawstring as you affirm that you take back your power and strength from the pain you feel.
6. Take this pouch with you every time it's that time of the month so you can feel better physically and bring balance to your emotions.

Third Eye Opening Spell

You need your third eye to help you to ride the hedge. The more open it is, the easier this experience will be for you, and the more profound your insights will be.

You'll Need:
- 1 drawstring bag (a small one)
- Some mugwort sprigs (make them fresh)
- Some chips of sandalwood

Steps:
1. Mix the sandalwood and mugwort, then use them to fill the drawstring pouch.

2. Lie comfortably, shut your eyes, and let the bag sit in the middle of your forehead, between your brows, and above eye level.
3. Take some calming deep breaths and let yourself release all thoughts and concerns.
4. In your mind's eye, see yourself become more spiritually awakened, enlightened, and open to communication with your divine self. See radiant white light as it flows from the universe, moving through the herbs in your pouch, going straight into your third eye, causing it to open even more.
5. Allow yourself to soak in the power of this radiant white light as you affirm that you have more wisdom and are in touch with your intuition. Affirm that your third eye is wide open and healthy.

Psychic Booster Amulet

If you want to be more in touch with your spirit guides and be able to hear when they have critical messages for you, then this is an amulet worth making and keeping on your person. As you continue to wear it, it will make it easier for you to access visions, gain wisdom, and receive insight from your ancestors and other guides you have.

You'll Need:
- 1 Teaspoon sage (dried)
- 1 Teaspoon cinnamon (ground)
- 1 Leather cord (at least 18 inches in length)
- Modeling clay

Steps
1. Roll a bit of modeling clay in your hands until it's soft and easy to manipulate.
2. Add sage and cinnamon, working them into the clay with your fingers while imagining you're opening up your heart and soul to receiving messages from the spirit. You can work the clay into a little circle or any other shape you like that is magically significant to you.
3. Let the clay dry, and then attach it to your cord or chain. This will make it easier for you to receive spiritual messages clearly.
4. Whenever you want to receive guidance about a specific message, you can hold this in your dominant hand as you say a prayer or set

an intention to receive insight on whatever topic is bothering you.

5. If you like, you can place this beneath your pillow at night while going to sleep, thinking about what you need guidance on. You will have dreams where your guide will communicate the answers you seek. It is important that you sleep with the mindset that you will definitely receive answers.

Conclusion

For many years, the author of this book practiced hedge witchcraft and, during the course of doing so, learned a great deal about trees, herbs, and plants and their nature. It was also possible to learn how they interact with the environment, which was not only an intriguing study but also a vital tool to aid her family and her community.

You may learn, as she did, some important life lessons from practicing hedge witchcraft. The first lesson is that learning anything new is never too late. You can reach a deep understanding of certain topics by learning, such as reading books, watching videos, attending classes, etc. There is no shortage of sources for learning your craft if you should choose to go down this path.

The second lesson is to think outside the box. There are so many tools and ways to learn that it can be helpful to pose questions within your family or circle of friends regarding what you have just learned. For example, what could you do with this newly acquired information? By asking these questions, you can grow and expand on your beliefs, or you'll see if someone else has already done something similar, which may lead to further learning or borrowing from their craft or practices.

Whatever you do, do not neglect the power of hedge riding. Use it to your advantage to communicate with guides and get higher knowledge about the secrets locked within certain herbs and plants and how you can best use them. There are more things to learn about these gifts of nature than any book on the planet could possibly teach you. Some plants may respond to you differently than how they would to another witch. So, use your hedge riding sessions to learn more about your craft from the wiser spirits.

Hedge witchcraft is a practice that teaches you to honor and respect the natural world (especially trees and plants) and people. It teaches you to be a part of the ecosystem and love what comes from the trees instead of simply taking from it. If you are ever in doubt, ask the plants or trees for permission to use what you need. There are many ways to conduct this sort of hedge witchcraft, and you can talk to the trees or plants, sing to them, whisper to them, or use a pendulum, divining rod, or rune staves.

Any method that allows you to communicate with the tree is acceptable. Simply put, it is a very personal practice - something that must be done on an individual level and not simply copied from someone else. So, if the herbs or your intuition tell you that you can use them for a certain intention, then feel free to do that. Make every spell and ritual your own because the power lies in your uniqueness.

Finally, you need to remember that this is a practice. In other words, reading is only one step. You have to actually craft spells and get in touch with your deity to see results. You can't read about one thing and decide you've mastered it. Put everything you learn here to the test, and if you don't succeed at first, that doesn't mean it doesn't work. Get clear in your intentions and try again; *never forget to record what you are doing in your grimoire.*

Part 2: Hedge Druidry

The Ultimate Guide to Druidism, Animism, Druid Magic, Celtic Spellcraft, Ogham, and Rituals of Solitary Druids

Introduction

In this book, we will fully explore Hedge Druidry, but you first need to understand what Druidry is - as *Hedge* Druidry is a branch of this wonderful spiritual path that we walk through life.

Not to confuse you, but Druids are many things. They are priests, messengers, scientists, philosophers, teachers, leaders, guides, and more. They are in tune with the natural and spiritual worlds and have connections to ancient monuments like Stonehenge. They believed in equality in all ways before it became a political issue in our modern world.

But Druidry is also a misunderstood and, at times, *confusing* philosophy. When not much is known about Druidry, people often misunderstand what Druidry is about. Do they incant spells during the full moon? Are they a cult that wears robes to conceal identities? Can Druids turn into animals? Movies and TV shows have portrayed Druidry in certain ways, and while much is true, there is a lot that is false.

I am here to set you on the right path by gaining knowledge and insight into what Druidry is and how you can apply that to your life in this modern world. You will start at the beginning with a quick history lesson, but don't worry; the information is only so that you can build on this knowledge to understand what being a Druid is really about.

Once you have the basics, we will quickly move on to the application, which is what this book is about. You will learn what it means to fully be a Druid and not just a Druid, but a *Hedge Druid*. You will then have the opportunity to start practicing what you know, including visiting the spiritual world and performing Druid magic.

This is a journey, and it begins with a single step. So, when you are ready, move onto the next page, and start your amazing Druid journey.

Chapter 1: From Druidry to Hedge Druidry

Let us start with Druidry in general before you dip your toes into the amazing world of Hedge Druidry.

What Is Druidry?

Let us start with a timeframe.

Druidry or Druids have been around for centuries. Although ancient Druidry is often thought of as male-dominated, Druids have always promoted gender equality. The modern understanding of Druids is men and women in long cloaks participating in clandestine meetings and rituals. While some of that might be true, true Druidry is not about the hidden but what is seen. Druidry has not changed much over the years, and while the cloaks might have been swapped for modern attire, cloaks were most likely worn because they were practical; a cloak on a cold night under the moon is an appropriate fashion choice.

Druids have been around for centuries.
https://pixabay.com/es/photos/magia-bosque-brujer%c3%ada-fantas%c3%ada-6585335/

When we think of Druidry, certain words often come to mind, spiritual, mystical, powerful, knowledge, and magic. Because of this, people are often wary. They believe that Druids are people with power, and we all know what power does to people, especially in our modern world. Don't worry! All you have heard about Druidry is true, just without the inclination for world domination or using their power negatively. And, after training and focusing, you can dip into the power and magic for yourself.

No one is quite sure where the word "Druid" comes from nor what the word means, and there are many possible translations. The most prominent theory is that the word is translated from an old Irish word meaning knowledge or wisdom. That would certainly fit with Druidry.

Religions of the world can be broken down into subcategories, theism, shamanism, paganism, etc. Druidry is a shamanistic religion. It is a religion that combines medical practices such as administering herbs and other natural medicines for sickness and illness and contacting nature and other spirits to aid in treatment. It is a religion rooted in the physical world, bound by universal laws and all the knowledge contained within, and in the spiritual world and the beings that are out of our sight and reach. In essence, it is a belief structure focused on knowledge; some of that knowledge is beyond what many people believe to be true. Thankfully, for us Druids, it is true, and you can use it to great benefit for the betterment of the world.

We do not know when Druidry first appeared, but we do know that it has been around for centuries. While Druidry might have been around for many, many millennia, we can date the first mention of Druidry to the second century BCE (before the Common Era). That is the first mention, so we can be sure that it was around for some time before that.

Druids were respected back then. Sadly, Druids are not as respected now as they were then, but that is down to the competing religions that have emerged over the two millennia since Druidry was prevalent. The shamanistic, pagan, and heathen religions promote a world of living in harmony and respecting the other religions. While other religions respect others as human beings, they often have no room for any belief in any other religion other than their own.

Go back one or two millennia, and Druids were leaders in every sense of the word. Not only did they connect people to the spirit world and the gods and goddesses, but they helped to guide people in our mortal plane. They were the scientists and philosophers of their day, and they were connected with the spirit world. They did not have beliefs based on faith alone but on knowledge and science. They would teach others, provide judgment when agreements could not be sought, and would even engage in peace talks when there was a war. It was a cyclical feedback loop. Druids were respected individuals, and because of this, they were able to negotiate, teach, and guide, but they gained that respect by being the most knowledgeable, by having a thirst to know the world, and by engaging in a constant search for meaning and wisdom.

So, when undertaking your journey into Hedge Druidry, you can start by bettering yourself. If you want to be a Druid, you aspire to be a teacher, a guide, an intermediary. To do this, you need to be knowledgeable, skillful, and the best person you can be. The best way to set out to be a Druid is through a path of self-betterment. But we'll revisit that later in this book. Back to the past!

Druidry is a theistic religion – yet a *polytheistic* one. Druids mostly believe, in multiple gods and goddesses, another example of gender equality in Druidry. When looking into Druidry, many people compare the polytheistic nature of the belief system to the Greek and Roman gods and beliefs. There are certainly similarities in terms of other-worldly beings.

Back to the robes . . . While we did mention that robes would be used on cold evenings in Britain, official Druids wore robes with colors that denoted rank or specialty. Golden robes, as you might guess, were worn by those held in the highest esteem, the wise leaders. Priests would wear white robes. Then there were robes for those who were soldiers, artists, builders, etc. Some media has the wearing of robes right, but they were not worn to conceal identity but to denote rank.

There is an organizational structure to Druidry. The Arch-Druid would be at the head with the priest below and other Druids below them. As has been described, wearing cloaks under the moon and the lunar calendar is certainly very important to Druids. As with most pagan, shamanic, and heathen religions, full moons are celebrated, and other holidays that fall on the equinoxes or planting of seeds and harvest times.

The Rituals, the Worship, and Stonehenge

Going back six thousand years, many stone structures, such as standing stone rings and henges, started to appear. Historians cannot say for certain whether these were built by Druids and used as places of worship, but there is a strong suggestion that Druidry has been around for a lot longer than is recorded in the written word.

Along with being a polytheistic religion, Druidry can be described as *animism*. Druids are characterized by a connection to nature and the spirit world that lies beyond. They are more interested in a holistic way of life that tries to live in harmony with nature, a difficult thing to do in our modern world. This means observing and interacting with nature. By looking at what is happening around you, you can often see what is coming. This could be by observing weather patterns, watching life cycles, or being in nature to better get in touch with oneself. Of course, we are only touching on the possibilities of nature as a Druid; later in this book, we'll delve into this more. You will also find spirit and animal guides in the world of Druidry, and they can guide and shape you too.

Druids follow the lunar calendar closely, and the solar calendar is also important. You can see this in the stone structures built many centuries ago, including Stonehenge. These places were seen as places of power, and, for the most part, the stone structures were built to align with the sun and moon. This was important when worshipping nature and provided a calendar or clock for the year. You can still go to many of these henges, stone circles, and other buildings at certain times of the year, such as the summer solstice, and see the sunrise or sunset lining up with the stone.

Stonehenge.
https://pixabay.com/es/photos/stonehenge-monumento-arquitectura-1590047/

Rituals and worship can be performed both solo and in groups. In its simplest form, a Druid ritual can be as easy as taking a walk in nature. The more people who are involved, the more structured the ritual usually becomes. Most of what it means to be a Druid is about aligning with nature. You can perform rituals and worship daily, but some larger celebrations fall around the solstices and other times of the year that are more formal. Food and drink are often consumed or used to honor the gods and goddesses.

If you delve deep into the world of Druidry, you will find that there are some really cool things you can do. Druidry is often portrayed as a mystical and spiritual religion, and this is true. With practice and some natural inclination toward the spiritual world, you can cast spells and even leave your body. Spells, walking the spiritual world, and many general rituals are used to be closer to nature and protect nature. Many people use their Druid powers to actively oppose what is happening to the world today. Thousands of years ago, they used those same powers to maintain balance and harmony in the world.

Christianity and Druidry

Druidry has been through a lot. It was once a prevalent polytheistic religion across much of Europe, but it sharply declined when Christianity flooded across the continent. We can plot Druidry within two specific time periods, pre-Christianity and post-Christianity. As there is not a lot of specific writing about Druidry before Christianity, it is hard to know whether or not Druidry today is the same as it was thousands of years ago or whether the religion has been rekindled and modern-day Druidry is a reinvention of the old beliefs.

We know that many theist religions borrow from pagan and shaman religions – or, at least, it looks that way. You only have to look at the celebrations taking place in many faiths to see that they fall on or around the solstices, the planting of crops, and harvest time. Many pagan gods and goddesses have been warped or combined to form the gods of the theistic religions we have today. The histories, mythologies, and practices are very similar. So, you could argue that Druidry was never wiped out or lying dormant but was always a part of life as part of other religions.

We also know that much of what is known about Druidry and the other polytheistic or animist religions was recorded by those who were Christians, so we have to take research from many different sources to uncover the true nature of Druidry. Much of what is known about Druidry millennia ago is confined to mythology, but that does not mean that we cannot know about it, learn from it, and allow it to shape our modern world.

Modern-day Druidry was born in the middle of the twentieth century. While modern-day Druidry revolves around the Celts, you can find examples of Druidry worldwide, suggesting that Druidry is a natural path to follow. You only have to look to the indigenous peoples of North America or Australia to see how listening to the land, nature, and following the calendar of the sun and moon can sustain a people for millennia. It is only when outside influences and beliefs are inserted that the way of life starts to fall apart. This is not a suggestion that we go back to that way of life; that would be impossible, no matter how hard we try. But there's good reason to advocate the practice of these ancient beliefs in our modern world. While Druids are not looked to for guidance and help, Druids can still practice their beliefs and influence the world.

So, before we get into Hedge Druidry, let us look at the main tenets of Druidry and how you can start on your own path.

The Three Druid Goals

Starting on a Druid path in the modern day is as simple as declaring yourself a Druid. You do not need to believe in a god or multiple gods or goddesses. Some Druids around the world describe themselves as atheists, Christians, Buddhists, and of other religions. But the common factor in all Druids is a belief in nature, and three common goals unite all Druids.

1. Wisdom

I have already mentioned that ancient Druids were looked to for their wisdom and knowledge. While you might not be looked to specifically for wisdom on a grand scale, you can still share wisdom with those around you. Wisdom comes from knowledge and experience. You can be in control of both. Knowledge is all around us. You could enlist in a school program, take courses, or just read more books. The more you search out knowledge, the more wisdom you will naturally have. And you can seek out experience too. Be around more people, do more things, and ask for help when you need it so you can help others. The more you do, the more wisdom you will attain. Wisdom also means knowing when not to help someone or when you do not have the skills to help.

2. Creativity

Druidry dates back millennia, long before the written word was used to record everything for posterity. Druidry was passed down through oral tradition and storytelling. Not only that, but Druidry was present in songs, poems, art, and more. Now that everything is readily available on the Internet, you do not need storytelling to pass down the knowledge of Druidry, but the oral tradition is still important for connection. And this is not only applicable to other people but to the animals and spirits too. By utilizing story, song, art, and other forms of creativity, you share with others, both worldly and other-worldly beings, and that fosters community.

3. Love

It gets without saying that love should play a bigger role in our world. Community and love are being lost with the separation of people through distances and enclosed homes. Love is understanding and is important when you are promoting Druidry. The goal of Druidry is not to impose your religion on others or even convert others to Druidry, but to love people and the world. By showing love, you will bring people to Druidry, and those who do not want to practice Druidry will be more inclined to practice the Druid way of life without becoming a Druid. And, let's face it, promoting love and loving people and the planet will make the world a better place.

What Is Hedge Druidry?

Finally, we get here. You have received your crash course on Druidry, so let us get into what makes Hedge Druidry different from Druidry and why you might want to practice Hedge Druidry.

We discussed *community* - which is very important in our modern world and irrelevant to the religion you practice. You should always strive to be surrounded by people who can help you and that you can influence, but not in a manipulative way, to better the world.

But, to the crux of the matter, a Hedge Druid is someone who practices Druidry alone.

Except for the more formal gatherings and rituals, all of the above information about Druidry applies to a Hedge Druid. However, practicing alone does not mean you cannot go to more formal gatherings to experience them.

There are many reasons to become a Hedge Druid, some forced and some chosen. One of the most common reasons is that you might live in an area with no other Druids. You might not have a Druidry community around you, which forces you to practice alone, which is totally fine. In this case, you might consider always practicing alone if you like it, or you might practice alone until a group forms, or you yourself form a group.

You might be a person who enjoys being alone. You might not want to practice with others and use Hedge Druidry as your alone time where you can go off into nature and be away from the world and people for a while. It might feel more comfortable for you to be a solo Druid, which is extremely valid. In fact, knowing this about yourself gives rise to a more powerful Druidry. If you join a community and do not like being around people all the time, you will not be able to truly practice Druidry. By being a Hedge Druid, because you know you will be your best self when practicing, you will be able to influence and better the world much more.

There are times when the world goes through change. As recently as 2020, and going further back to the early 1900s, there have been worldwide pandemics. You might not want to be around other people for medical reasons, and you might have personal reasons. Any reason that makes you more comfortable in your spiritual path is a good reason to become a Hedge Druid.

You might not want to antagonize the people around you. Suppose you have grown up in a very religious family, and they are practicing today. In that case, you might not want to anger them by actively pursuing your religion. While this does not suggest hiding who you are, there are specific instances where doing so is beneficial. If you can practice your religion while not alienating yourself from your community, you are going to be happier in life.

And, while you are practicing alone, that does not mean you cannot have community. You will most likely have a community around you, even if they are not practicing Druids, and you can still have an online community. While you practice alone, you can still correspond with other Druids by email or regular mail.

To state it simply, a Hedge Druid is a Druid who practices alone. There are many reasons to do so, and all are equally valid. If you are the best Druid you can be, you are following the right path.

Chapter 2: The Awen and Celtic Cosmology

Do you want to become a Hedge Druid and practice Druidry by yourself? Before you walk the Druidic path, you need to know about the elements of the cosmos as a whole, so you can better ground yourself in them. Two concepts of Druidry that are best to start with are the Awen and Celtic cosmology.

The Awen

Many religions talk about the spirit. The Chinese have chi, India has the chakras, and there are many other religions and cultures that describe a central topic of human life in the same way.

To put it simply, the Awen is the energy of the universe. As mentioned briefly in the introduction, we will discuss two concepts in this chapter. While the Awen is all around us, let's consider taking Awen as the energy we find inside and the Celtic cosmology as the world outside the body. While the Awen does exist around us in the cosmos, it affects us from within.

You can think of the Awen as an energy that is always omnipresent, but at the same time, it is a flow. The Awen flows through us, and we flow through the Awen. This might sound mysterious and incomprehensible, and it is not our intention to confuse or muddle. The Awen is a great and powerful thing, and in many ways, you do not need to understand it to utilize it. How can we understand a flow of energy that channels through us to help us accomplish deeds without being able to measure or categorize it? We cannot. *But we can feel it, and we will use it.*

Using the Awen is about being. You are alive, and the Awen flows through you. Sometimes, you might not even notice it. You might find yourself suddenly inspired to burst into song or create something, and you have the Awen to thank for that. But it is much more than just accidental. You can meditate with the Awen, be conscious of it as you go about your day, and channel it to better inspire creativity and greatness.

The act of mindfulness is a great way to use the Awen. While it does flow through you and help you, by being mindful and deliberate about what you are thinking and doing, you can use it with purpose. Using the Awen, you are becoming more at one with nature and the surrounding world. Just be mindful that, like anything in life, practice makes perfect. You will not be able to harness the full power of the Awen just because you say you are a Druid. You need to first follow the Druid way of life and practice it. The more you practice, the more the Awen will flow through you.

How Do We Define the Awen?

Druidry is about wisdom, creativity, and love. When we think of the Awen, we can define it through our creativity. Of course, it will influence the other two goals also, but it is in our creativity that it will really shine. Many cultures have muses both in mythology and the present day. A muse inspires creativity in someone else or in multiple people. We can define the Awen as a muse, but not a physical one. As the Awen is also a flow, we could say that the essence of a muse is flowing through the world (if that makes sense). You can also think about it as inspiration. When inspiration strikes, that is the Awen. These concepts are all rooted in the world we know, so it becomes hard to define exactly what the Awen is, but we can compare it to the concepts we know.

We can describe the Awen as divine inspiration, being something above what we can comprehend. As it is not connected to a specific deity, although you can also experience divine inspiration, it is fine to also refer to it as just inspiration. All of this is a long way to describe the creative force that is the Awen.

We can be sure that the Awen has been a firm fixture of the Druid religion for a long time and is not an invention of modern Druidry. There is mention of it in multiple sources that date back many centuries. The

Awen is also described as your creative life force in ancient writings. You are alive, and the Awen wants to work through you. The Awen is the creative force that is begging to be released.

How Can You Use the Awen?

Although the term bard is mostly confined to dungeons and dragons, it was a common term in ancient Druidry. As mentioned, Druidry was a religion and way of life passed down through the generations through storytelling, songs, and poems. If you have ever sat through an awful movie, listened to a bland song, or endured a boring lecture, the correlation between the entertainment value of a presented work and the amount of information retained is very telling. In ancient times, bards were a very important part of the oral traditions, and they could pass on information in an entertaining and informative way. Bards were revered in ancient Druidry, and they were bestowed with the Awen. That is right; the Awen can also be bestowed by someone else or something else, usually a potion or a spell.

Bards were important in ancient times, and while they are not called by name today, they are still important, and a bard is something you might strive to be. While we do not need bards to pass down Druidic knowledge (though they still can), we do need bards to enhance the world. It has been shown that in every culture, both new and old, art is important to the advancement of society.

If you feel naturally inclined toward the bardic life, you can focus your time more on the Awen. You might already naturally have more Awen within you, and you can also meditate with the Awen to better write songs, stories, and more. When you use this inspiration to create works of art, you will make the world a better place, and even if you are not conveying the information of Druidry, you are sure to be conveying something of importance.

Finding the Awen in Nature

Whenever we talk about Druidry, we always come back to nature. Nature is an important and integral part of Druidry, and if you want to seek out the Awen, there is no better place than nature. Have you ever been out for a walk or being in nature when inspiration has struck? Do you always have your best ideas when walking among the trees? Or listening to the sound of the waves lapping on the shore? That is the power of the Awen.

Druidry can be used to bestow bardic inspiration on someone by spells or potions, but the easiest and most readily available way to find the Awen is to venture into nature. It takes practice to bestow the Awen, so get out of the house and take a walk in nature. Go on, do it now! As you take your walk, be more mindful of your surroundings. Listen, see, taste, touch, and smell. Take in everything around you, looking around and up as you do. Feel the sun or breeze on your face. Listen to the birds or grasshoppers. Taste a wild raspberry. Touch the bark of a tree or the soft grass. Be in nature and wait for inspiration to hit. And do not worry if it does not; simply enjoy being in nature and wait for inspiration to strike the next time.

Venturing into nature is imperative to finding the Awen.
https://unsplash.com/photos/78A265wPiO4

You can also take your creative works with you. Sitting by the window at home at your desk and composing a poem or sketching is fine, but when you take your work out into nature, you will benefit from the Awen. Set up an easel and paint what you see outside, or take your journal and do some free writing where you write down whatever comes into your head without thinking about it.

The Awen can be unpredictable, and the flow might come like a gentle stream or a strong river. But the key thing to keep in mind is that the Awen is a flow. It flows where it wants and does not want to become blocked. If a river is blocked, it will find a way around. So, if you block the Awen, it will find a way to flow around you. This means that as the Awen flows into you, you must also let it out. When you feel inspired, do something with it. If you have a great idea for a story, start jotting it down. If you feel like painting, do it. If you want to start singing, start singing. The more you let the Awen flow from you as it flows in, the more the flow will find you. And, to take the water metaphor further, you need to let it flow where it wants. If you feel inspired to sing, it might be okay to compose some song lyrics instead of singing a song, but you shouldn't use that inspiration to paint instead. Do not block the Awen, and let the Awen flow where it needs to go.

The more you work with the Awen, the more it will work with you. So, you should not only let it flow through you but actively seek it when you need it.

The Awen Chant and Cultivating Awen

You can find The Awen in nature, but you can chant the word to invoke the Awen when you are in nature or anywhere else. This is one of the first things you will learn as a Druid; all you need is the correct pronunciation.

Druidry has deep roots in Welsh, Irish, and Celtic cultures. The pronunciation of words can be a little different from how they are written, and it might be a good time to learn how to pronounce the word "Awen."

Awen is broken down into three syllables, "Ah," "Oh," and "En." Put all three syllables together, and you have "Awen." Chanting the word is a little different from just saying it. You want to take a deep breath and say each syllable loudly, surely, and confidently. You should chant it as often as feels natural to you or as often as it takes to feel connected with the Awen. You don't necessarily need to chant it; you can sing it too. If you are singing it, you can dance as you do.

When you are chanting or singing the word, be mindful of what you are saying and why you are saying it. You should be focused on the Awen and accepting it into your person. Think about why you need inspiration and what that inspiration will bring. Go out into nature and chant proudly. When you feel the Awen flowing through you, be sure to do something with it.

You can also invoke the Awen by using the Awen symbol, three rays of light emanating downward and out, tapered at the top and slightly spread apart. Many Druids wear Awen necklaces or bracelets or have Awen glass in their windows so the sunlight can shine through them. This is especially potent if you place one in your work area to help cultivate creativity.

Be mindful that you will not find inspiration if there are distractions. This can come in many forms, but common distractions come internally and externally. If you constantly tell yourself that you are not creative, that you cannot do something, that your work is not very good, inspiration will not come. This is a process, and it needs time. You are not setting out to become the best at something but to improve yourself, no matter how big or small. The same goes for the people you surround yourself with. If they are constantly putting you down, the Awen will not flow. When you are channeling the Awen, limit the distractions. Nature is perfect as there are usually not a lot of distracting noises and no TV on to snare your gaze.

Try to channel the Awen into every aspect of your life. You do not need to channel the Awen and then compose a musical masterpiece or paint the Mona Lisa. If you are playing with your children, use the inspiration in your games. If you need to plan a trip, be creative with it. Try to find ways to channel the Awen so the Awen opens itself up to you more.

The Celtic Cosmos

The Awen might be everywhere in the universe, but we're more concerned with how it flows through our person. When we look to the Awen, we look inside ourselves. But what about the bigger picture? What can the known universe tell us about ourselves, and how can you use it when you walk the path of Hedge Druidry?

The Wheel

Many cultures take the symbol of the wheel or the circle as one of their main symbols. There is an obvious reason for this. When we think of a circle, we think of one continuous line that goes around and around, a line with no beginning and no end. For most cultures, the idea of a life without end is one worth gripping onto, and we can also find many instances of circular rhythms in daily life. The seasons follow the same pattern, moving around and around like a wheel. Day follows night, and night follows day. The stars move around our plant as if on a giant wheel.

Wheel of the year.
Midnightblueowl, CC BY-SA 3.0 <https://creativecommons.org/licenses/by-sa/3.0>, via Wikimedia Commons https://commons.wikimedia.org/wiki/File:Wheel_of_the_Year.JPG

The wheel is an important symbol in Druidry. It can mean many things; as mentioned, it pertains to day and night, the stars, and the seasons. As a Druid, you will also come to know that it symbolizes life and death. It was believed that when you died, you would reside among the stars, the great wheel that constantly turns around us.

The number three is considered a magic number, and we can find that number all around us, and not just in major religions. There is life, death, and the in-between. It takes two adults to make a child making three people. Because of this, you will often find circles or wheels in groups of three. Spirals, too, are the natural expansion of the circle, a circle that continues to emanate outward with no end.

The four seasons divide the wheel that was the year, constantly turning around us. The sun and moon were important to the Celts, and they based their calendar on the moon. Instead of twelve months in a calendar year, they had thirteen, the number of full moons yearly. The seasons were the same, and there were festivals associated with the beginning of each season, especially summer and winter, where the wheel would be turned to its opposing side.

The Druidry of ancient times was linked to nature, and as a massive part of life was growing food that could be consumed, a large focus on nature was at both planting and harvest. This carries forward to today in some of the festivals and holidays.

We can open ourselves up to the cosmos to better celebrate the world around us and nature. When we look to the stars and seasons, we know how nature will react, which helps us better plan our trips into nature to find the Awen.

The Three Realms: Sea, Land, and Sky

Ancient Druids believed that three separate realms lived in harmony and existed together. They also represented the three elements of the world, and it was believed that everything was made up of these three elements. *Everything,* the lands of our cosmos - and the beings within - can all be explained as a combination of either sea, land, or sky. It can be helpful to think of the three lands as more than just what we can see. The sea is below our world, the land is the earth we live on, and the sky is above us, both seen and unseen.

1. The Sea

We can see some of the sea realms, and when it comes to explaining the world, it can be compared to the water element. But the sea realm does not only extend to what we can see in front of us. The seas and oceans access the sea realm and reside deep within the earth. We can think of the sea realm as a sort of underworld, but not in the typical sense of heaven and hell. The dead go there, so our ancestors are there, and it makes sense that not all of our ancestors would go to hell. There is no distinction in where they go, and it is not a good or bad place, just a place for those who have passed to reside.

The fairies also live in this world. If you want to give offerings to the fairies or your ancestors, you can do so through the water. This can be any body of water and does not need to be confined to the sea and ocean.

Food, drink, and flowers are common offerings for fairies and ancestors. To give the offering, simply drop the offering into the water while being mindful of the ecosystem you are disturbing.

2. The Land

The land is our world, but it is more than that. It is everything contained within, everything that Mother Nature has given us. This includes us, the plants and flowers, the trees, rocks, mountains, streams, rivers, and everything else. If you are looking for a place of power or a place where the Awen is more plentiful, look for elements in the land realm that touches on another realm. For example, mountains are buried deep in the ground but reach up and touch the sky. Some plants live both in the land and water, and the land is comparable to the earth's elements.

You can use wine, tobacco, honey, and other foods as offerings to powerful liminal artifacts in the earth realm. As the oak tree is a powerful symbol within Druidry, you can give offerings to oak trees. Still, anything that is living between two worlds can be given an offering. It is thought that giving offerings this way can help you travel between worlds.

3. The Sky

The sky realm is what you can see above, but it is also the realm of the gods and goddesses, such as the thunder god or the battle goddess. There are also solar and lunar deities. The sky is associated with the air element, but the sun is also in the sky, so you can equate it with the fire element.

Many deities are honored with fire. The great ball of fire, the sun, burns in the sky, giving life, and the smoke from the fire also travels up to the sky to where the gods reside.

Trees and the Three Realms

As mentioned above, some things in our world can touch all three worlds at the same time. Trees are a prime example. They reach down and touch the sea realm, they are in the earth realm, and their branches and leaves reach up to touch the sky realm. In ancient Druid times, trees were worshipped. Rituals were held there, oaths were sworn under trees, and every tribe had a sacred tree.

As a Hedge Druid, you can also have a sacred tree. It does not need to be a specific tree, though oak, ash, and elm are preferred. You might be drawn to a specific tree or several trees. Spend time under the tree/trees, performing rituals and rites, or just meditating beneath the boughs.

Chapter 3: Opening Your Mind to Nature

As you might have gathered by now, nature plays a large role in Hedge Druidry. You can find the Awen by visiting nature, but it is about a lot more than that. Being a Druid is about connecting with nature, protecting nature, and using nature to better explore yourself and the world, bettering yourself as you do. When you start to explore nature, your powers as a Druid will start to expand. But, before we talk about some of the powerful things nature can bring you, let us go back to one of Druidry's three main goals: wisdom.

Your path as a Druid should be focused on improving wisdom in all areas, but it is especially important to do so with nature. The more you know about nature, the more wisdom you will have, and the more you can help the world and others. When starting as a Druid, it's recommended that you focus on nature to better prepare yourself for becoming a true Druid.

The Wisdom Found in Nature

You want to know as much as possible about the natural world around you, and that means knowing what nature is, how it reacts, and what it does. While you can learn a lot from books and other forms of media, there is no better way to get to know nature than to be out in it. And there is the added benefit that you can tap into the Awen while you are in nature.

You can still read about nature and explore that world. After all, some things are not passed down by oral tradition, and you could harm yourself if you go out into nature and eat some poisonous mushrooms or taste the wrong berry. So, unless you have a Druid bard with you, do your research before you engage fully.

Some things cannot be learned from books, and by being in nature, you are going to learn about them. For example, a trail running through the woods might be close to your home made by deer. You might notice that the bark of a tree is eaten in a certain spot. You might see how a river affects the landscape around it when it floods. By observing nature and studying it, you can piece together how the ecosystem around you works. And, when you know nature, you know how to help it.

When you have studied nature for a while and read up on any concepts you are unsure about, you should try to understand it. There is a big difference between having knowledge and understanding it; you could compare having knowledge with having wisdom. If the deer do make a path through a certain area, why do they? And if the river swells and adapts to the landscape, what does that do to the overall ecosystem? By looking for understanding, you will also find the paths of energy that run through nature, enabling you to better find the Awen.

Recording your findings and thoughts is a good habit to get into. By the time you get home, you might have forgotten about something, and over time, that "something" could form a pattern. If you find a particularly inspiring tree, you can add it to your book and even draw it if the inspiration strikes. You can write warnings to yourself so you do not make the same mistakes over and over again. Perhaps part of the grass is growing, and you want to ensure it is not trampled on. Or you can sketch some flowers that might be edible so you can check on them when you get home. Be curious. Always ask questions and see if you can discover the answer by observing. Of course, wisdom knows where to look for the answer when you do not have it.

As a Hedge Druid, you will constantly be interacting with nature. This means building on your knowledge and wisdom of nature before and after you are in it. It also means using nature to live your life. There is great wisdom to be found by directly interacting with nature.

Druids used to live within nature and take from it what they needed to live. We have lost these old ways, though they are coming back to life through Druidry and a need to go back to a simpler life that does not harm the environment. When interacting with nature, it is wise to learn the skills needed to interact with nature properly.

You want to help nature, but that does not mean you cannot take from it. It means that you should not take more than you need, and you should also ensure that you are not damaging the ecosystem when you take. This involves knowing the life cycle of plants and animals, knowing which plants and animals you use, and limiting your waste. You want to look for beneficial exchanges. For example, suppose there is an abundance of raspberries. In that case, you can do other plants and animals a favor by harvesting some of the fruits and cutting down the stalks for ground cover against the harsh sun (and to lock in moisture).

You should also engage with nature in different ways to help you discover parts that you would not normally see. So, get out there and do some rock climbing or bouldering, kayak or canoe down a river or across a lake, and engage in outdoor activities all year round, such as skiing.

You will find that by being out in nature, you will become more attuned to it, which is important for the next parts of your Hedge Druid journey, rituals, and altars.

Nature Rituals and Altars

One of the first things you will physically do as a Druid is to build an altar. When you start, you have two options: building an altar in your home or building one outdoors. (It's a good idea to do both.) You can build an altar in your home, but as you try to converse with nature as much as possible, you should also go out into nature and build an altar in a place that has meaning to you or to which you feel some connection.

As with any time spent in nature, be sure to interact with it in a way that does not damage the delicate ecosystem.

Creating an altar is a chance for you to give offerings to your ancestor and spirit allies; we'll talk more about this in the next chapter about helping you contact them. If you are creating an altar indoors, it will most likely stay the same, but an outdoor altar can be created wherever you feel it is needed. It does not need to be permanent, and you can move your altar from spot to spot as you see fit. Change plays a large role in the life of a Druid, and we track changes through the year with different festivals and rituals. Your altar will change too. As you evolve, the spirits and ancestors you worship will change, too, so do not be afraid to change your altar when needed.

When you set out into nature to create your altar, the first thing to do is to use your senses and explore with mindfulness. The place for your altar is out there; all you need to do is find it. And a quick note on building altars in nature. If you are new to Druidry, spend a lot of time in nature before you begin to think about building an altar; take the time to learn and observe before you venture out to find the perfect place.

There is no way to tell you where the perfect place for your altar is. Tap into the Awen, and you will know when you have found the perfect spot. The ancestor(s) or spirit guide(s) you are honoring will play a part in the location, which is why an altar in nature makes sense.

If you take my suggestion to spend time in nature before considering building an altar, the places you might build one will most likely show themselves to you first. But be mindful of the seasons as you plan your altar. Your altar might be in a different place during the summer and winter – and the items placed on your altar will vary with the seasons.

When you find your place, you can set about with the creation of your altar. The altar does not have to be big, and you can make it as simple or as complicated as you want. Think about what you are trying to convey and who or what you are honoring. The seasons will help you decide what to place, which could mean fresh berries in summer, fallen bird's nests in winter, fallen leaves in autumn, or fruit that naturally fell from a tree.

When you are taking from nature the item for your altar, one thing to consider is whether your presence is welcome and if the spirits are allowing you to take the items. Sit with the item, thank the spirits around you for the gift, and listen for any response. It might be hard at first, but over time, you will be able to hear or feel the responses.

When you create an altar inside, you will have items from nature, but you will also include personal items, especially for an ancestor altar, and you can take items out into nature too. For example, if you are honoring an ancestor, you can take a picture of them to place on your altar. You might also bring items belonging to the person, drawings, food offerings, and other meaningful items.

When putting the altar together, you need to listen to the voice inside. You are honoring your ancestor or spirit, not invoking them. You do not need to have items that will necessarily bring them to you as long as you honor them well. For example, adding beauty to your altar shows honor, so items like petals, colorful fruit, and unique leaves will show that you are trying to set up an altar that looks good to honor the person or being. It is the thought that counts, and if you put thought into your altar, it will work.

When you have built your altar, sit with it, and think of the person or spirit you are honoring. This is a great way to connect yourself to nature and a specific person or being. And, when you practice your Druidry, you might feel a presence when you have an altar built.

When you are done, do not forget to clean up after yourself.

A Basic Druid Ritual

I will explore rituals more in a later chapter, but a good place to start as a beginner Druid is to perform a gratitude ritual for the nature around you. This is a simple ritual that does not require many components to get started. The components are easy to acquire if you do not already have them. This is a ritual that you can perform over and over to honor nature, and you can adapt the words used in this ritual to better fit who you are and how you want to honor nature. The included words are a guide and not a stipulation.

1. Find a place in nature where you can perform your ritual. This could be a place you have visited many times or a place you feel drawn to. Perhaps a place of power or somewhere where the Awen flows freely. As with most Druid practices, listen to your intuition. If you find that you know the place to hold the ritual, it is the right place for you.
2. Either ring a bell or clap your hands. This not only helps you to focus on the start of the ritual, but it invites the spirits.
3. Give a few words to announce the start of the ritual: "Spirits around me, gods and goddesses who look over me, mother nature who gives me what I need to live, I light this candle in your honor."
4. Light a candle.
5. Take ten deep breaths to clear your mind and purify your body.
6. Honor Mother Earth: "Earth mother, you give all that I see around me, and I am thankful that you do. Without you, there would be no life. I will return to your when my life comes to an end, and I will be transformed anew."
7. Share the blessing: *"I invite my ancestors to be here with me for they have enjoyed nature too, and they are now a part of the great life cycle."* You can invite any of the gods, goddesses, or spirits to share in the ritual with you.

8. Give an offering. In the simplest form, you can bring some food and drink. Try to match your offering to what the ancient Druids might have used, so instead of bringing candy and pop, you might bring a small glass of wine and some bread.
9. Thank whoever you invited to the ritual, in this case, your ancestors.
10. Thank Mother Earth.
11. End the ritual: *"I end this ritual."*

This might seem like a lot of steps to follow, but you will find that they are quite simple and quick to perform. You can use this ritual to honor the gods and goddesses, spirit allies, elemental powers, and just about everything else.

Druid Meditation Walks and Mindfulness

Meditation is a great way to temporarily escape from the world, and it is something that should be practiced by everyone, and not only Druids. Walking meditation allows us to get into nature and be mindful, and you do not even need to plan time specifically for this ritual. You are going to be in nature regularly, so meditate while you are out there.

Before we talk about how you meditate in nature, knowing why you are meditating is a good idea. The most common reason to meditate is to clear your mind. You can do this to unburden yourself of any stress, tension, or problems you are carrying. This meditation also helps you better manage your problems and sometimes find the answers you need. You can also meditate to be more mindful. If you find it hard to connect with nature, you can practice meditation to harness your connection. When people talk about mindfulness while in nature, we can substitute meditation as another way of viewing it. The third reason is to gain more focus. Suppose you are having trouble concentrating either in nature or at home. In that case, meditating can help to focus your mind so you can attend to the task at hand.

So, how do you meditate and walk at the same time?

When people think about meditation, they think about sitting cross-legged with their eyes closed and chanting. While this is a valid form of meditation, it is not the Druid meditation that you will do as you walk in nature, although you can find a comfortable spot and meditate like that too.

As with every meditation, your posture is important. You might not notice your posture as you walk but focus on your body and ensure that you are walking at a comfortable pace and that your back and shoulders are straight. Do not force a walking position; you should be comfortable as you walk, which will help your breathing.

The final part of the puzzle is to walk through nature and connect with it. Use your intuition to choose the best walking path and try to find a place where you are not likely to be disturbed. You can tap into the Awen for more inspiration as you complete your nature walk.

All you need to do on this walk, which is easier said than done, is experience everything around you. When you hear something, zone in on it and look for it. Can you hear a bird chirping? Stop and listen to it. Move your eyes and head around slowly and try to find the bird. Can you hear a stream? Follow the stream, dip your hand into it, and wash your face in it. Bend down and smell the flowers you would usually pass by. Run your hand over the different types of bark you pass and notice how they feel. Interact with the natural world around you and feel how it is different from when you are walking through unaware and unobservant.

Two Bonus Meditations

You do not always have to walk while you meditate in nature. A good meditation to help clear your mind is to use a noise distraction. This could be a running river, the wind through leaves, a tweeting bird, or any pleasant nature sound you can focus on for a period of time. Stand, sit, or lie near the sound and listen to it as you breathe in and out. If your mind wanders, bring it back to the sound of whatever you are focused on. You can take as much time as you want with this meditation.

You can also meditate to find inspiration with the Awen. Use your intuition once more to find the perfect place to inspire you. When you go out for this meditation, bring with you what you want to be inspired in. For example, if you want to write a poem, bring a pen and paper with you. Stand in the chosen place and look around you while taking some deep breaths. Start the Awen chant taught in the previous chapter, open your mind and be receptive to receiving your inspiration. Look around you, taking in your surroundings and using mindfulness to be in nature. Hold in your mind the inspiration you are looking for, and meditate for as long as you need.

Trees and Meditation

The word Druid is certainly synonymous with wisdom, and some scholars suggest that a translation of the word could be "wisdom of the oak" or "knowledge of the oak." Trees are important in the Druid world, and you will often find the tree symbol around Druids and Druidry. You will also find the tree symbol in many other religions; the tree of life is a good example. Trees are all about growth and branching off, an apt metaphor for life, both a single-life and a family tree. So, when you are meditating, you can incorporate trees to boost the power of meditation.

Trees help in focusing your meditation.
https://unsplash.com/photos/Hzbq4de24kQ

If you are in nature, you are likely going to be around trees, but you can also seek out trees (large oak trees are best) and sit at the bottom of them to meditate or build your altar at their base. And, as long as you are careful, you can become a more carefree and fun Druid by climbing a tree to observe nature from another angle.

Chapter 4: Meet Your Spirit Allies

There are two types of spirit allies we'll discuss in this chapter, which are split into these main topics: the spirits that passed from this world to the next, your ancestors, and the other spirits that belong to the many worlds, the fairies, nature spirits, animals, etc.

All are powerful in their own ways, and we'll see how you can harness the power of both types, how to meditate on them, and touch on some astral travel.

Connecting with Your Ancestor Allies

In the world of Druidry, your ancestors are defined a little differently, and we can split our ancestors into three categories. We have our ancestors in the typical sense of the word, that is, those who were related to us by blood. This could be a great grandfather or a great, great aunt. If you are a direct descendant of someone else, then they are your ancestor.

There are two other types of ancestors that you can call on too, ancestors of place and ancestors of tradition. Your ancestors of place are people who lived in the same place as you. For example, you might be from Scotland, or more specifically, the Scottish Highlands. Your ancestors of place might be the other Highlanders from Scotland. They are the people you feel connected to through the place in which you live. Your ancestors of tradition and people who share similar values and traditions as you do. The most obvious ancestors of tradition would be other Druids. Because you have lived your life the same way they have, you might feel a deep connection to them. When looking toward ancestors of tradition, you might find yourself looking upon a person who directly inspired your life. Many people have inspired us throughout their lifetimes, and we could take Martin Luther King Jr as an example of one. If you find yourself inspired by him and share similar values, you might call him an ancestor of tradition.

There are many reasons to honor and connect with your ancestors. The most common is to thank them for your being here. When you think about it, you can thank all three types of ancestors for your being here. If it were not for your blood ancestors, if one link in the chain were broken, you would not be physically present in this world. If it were not for your ancestors of place, you might not be here either. Many ancestors of place fought wars to maintain their homeland, and you might not have a place to live if it were not for them. The same is true of your ancestors of tradition. You might be physically here without them, but not in the same way. Without them fighting for their beliefs and carrying on traditions, you would be a different person and walking a different path. You should honor all three types of ancestors.

But that does not mean that you should honor everyone who came before you. When you are honoring your ancestors, it is important to focus. The most common way to honor and connect with your ancestors is to create a shrine. If you were to create a shrine to all of your ancestors at the same time, it would be overloaded, and the honor would be watered down. So, when it comes time to venerate your ancestors, think about the ancestors who are most important to you, the ones whom you want to walk with you on your path, and the ones you feel most connected to.

Creating an Ancestor Shrine or Altar

I spoke earlier about creating an altar in nature to honor the ancestors or spirits, but this shrine or altar is going to be a permanent fixture in your home and an altar that you can go to whenever you want. A key thing here is to be adaptable. Once you have your altar or shrine, do not be afraid to change it. If you find that an object is not working on the shrine, then you can switch it out. Or, if you want to remove an ancestor from your altar, go ahead and do that.

When you have your altar created, you might find that some objects work for some ancestors and not others. It is fine to make changes. You might also find out information about some ancestors that changes your perception of them, and you can remove them from your altar and add others. Remember, the ancestor that will help to guide you will almost never be malevolent, and they will not give you their life details. All we can use is what we know about them from what is recorded.

You can create a shrine or an altar; both are similar in creation. A shrine is a place where the ancestors are honored and remembered, while an altar is a place where you can perform rituals, such as ancestor meditation. When you are setting up your altar or shrine, take this into account. A shrine does not need much space, while an altar might need space in front for you to sit and meditate. Find a place in your home where you can honor your ancestors, and try to choose a place that is not out of the way. If you are honoring your ancestors, you do not want to place a shrine or altar in a cupboard. It is much better to have your altar in a place that you will visit regularly throughout the day.

Once you have your location, you can start to place items. Your actual altar could be a table, but it can also be something as simple as a shelf. Any flat surface will do, but remember that you are creating a place to honor and worship, so you will not use the floor for your altar. That being said, if you have a nice spot in your home where you can place items and sit to meditate, go for it. The key is to think about what is right for your altar and use your intuition.

When you have chosen your spot, you can use some of the following items to create your altar or shrine:

- A skull or bones to represent all of your ancestors/death as a whole.

- Photographs or pictures of your ancestors. It is important that you never use photos or pictures of those who are still alive on your altar or shrine.

- **Personal Items:** This can be left up to the individual, and the objects will vary from person to person. Think about what connects you most to an ancestor. Examples are watches, a pipe, clothing, jewelry, coins, and other personal items.

- **Powerful Stones:** Moonstone, quartz, and emerald are particularly potent for boosting your psychic energy when communing with the dead. Over time, you might find that you work better with different stones, so always be ready to adapt to what works best.

- **Offerings:** You can give offerings when you meditate or contact your ancestors, so you should have a plate and cup on the shrine or altar ready to be filled.
- **Earth:** You can place the earth in a container of your choice, but be sure it fits with your altar. A Mason jar will be nicer than a Tupperware container. The earth reminds us of where we came from and where we will return.
- **Water:** Depending on the location of your altar, you can keep the water in a sealed or unsealed container. A jar will work to seal it, and you might use a glass or metal cup if you want to leave it unsealed. Water helps us to focus our psychic energy.
- **A Candle:** You will light the candle when worshipping or communing; this not only illuminates our altar or shrine but helps us focus when we visit it.
- **Wand/Dagger:** You can use this item to direct your energy when you are at your altar. You will use this more on an altar than a shrine.
- **Deity Statue:** A statue of a deity of the dead or afterlife will help to guide the spirits. It does not need to be a statue; it can be a representation of that deity or an item associated with them.

Ancestor Meditation

Now that you have your altar, it is time to meditate with your ancestors. Do not worry if you do not have space for an altar and only have a shrine, and you will still be reaping the benefits. With everything in life, it is about thought and intention. If you only have space for a shrine and have done your best, your ancestors will walk with you through life.

Here is a step-by-step guide on ancestor meditation:
1. Always start every meditation by getting comfortable. You can sit or lie beside your altar, as long as you are in a position that will allow your mind to wander. You should also be in a place that is free of distractions.
2. Take some deep breaths to relax further. Breathe in and out three times, focusing on your breath.
3. Close your eyes and state your intent: "I want to meet my grandfather." The statement of intent can be anything you want

and wording in any way you like. You might want advice, help, wisdom, community, etc.

4. Visualize a journey down into the earth. If you remember from a previous chapter, your ancestors are in the sea realm under the earth. Think of yourself passing down into the earth, either by a cave or tunnel or anything else that helps you to make the journey down toward your ancestor.

5. Continue to breathe in a steady rhythm.

6. Eventually, you come to a cave or a tunnel deep underground. There is still living down here, a life that the sun cannot touch. You find a candle in your hand that lights your way and makes you feel safe. There is no danger down here. Walk down the path and continue to focus on your breathing.

7. You find a door at the end of the tunnel. When you open it, you find yourself in a place chosen by your ancestor, a place that makes sense for them to be. You might see your ancestors there or some form of representation of them. It could be a feeling that they are there with you.

8. Re-state your intent. Announce why you are there, and ask the spirits to help you. Ask the negative spirits to pass you by. Take in the surrounding area, and look for your ancestor. They might appear different from how you remember or envisage them. They have likely been on a journey in the afterworld and gained more wisdom.

9. Be with them. Fulfill the reason for your visit, whatever that might be.

10. When you are done, travel back the way you came, taking your time and focusing on your breathing.

11. When you are done, open your eyes again.

This is a more complex meditation than the one you did while walking in nature, and you might find that you do not get anything the first time. You might not get anything the first half-dozen times. Do not worry. With practice, the meditation will come to you, and you are strengthening your psychic abilities each time you practice. You were not able to ride your bike or master any other activity at the first attempt, but it came over time.

This is your first dip into the astral plane. When you visit your ancestors, you are moving from this world into the next. The first step is to make sure you are connecting with your ancestors before you travel to the astral plane. Creating your altar or shrine is the best way to do this. Maintain your altar or shrine and visit it regularly, so your ancestors are more receptive when you go to visit them.

Getting to Know Your Spirit Guides

There are many different spirit guides in the Druid world. Druidry is all about nature, and nature will help to guide us. We can further break down the spirits outside our ancestors into three categories: plant, animal, and fae. Plants are plants, animals are animals, and fae is the spirits that live beyond the veil of our world. You'll learn to gain a connection with each so they can guide you when you are traveling beyond this world and help you when you are in this one.

Plant Spirits

When it comes to communication with plants, there are many ways to do so. You do not necessarily need to talk to them and hear a response. You might talk with them and not get a response. You might be able to hear them but not talk to them. You could read their energy or emotions, be able to read the plants intuitively, use tools to interpret the plants or read the omens and signs the plants are giving off.

Or you might start out with nothing, and that is okay. Druidry is a journey; unless you are imbued with these skills already, you will have to learn them. Some people can naturally commune with the spirits in some ways, but most cannot. So, how do you better commune with the plant spirits? You immerse yourself in nature, of course. The more time you spend in nature, the more you are going to connect with the plant spirits.

As you develop your skills by being in nature, you will find that you are more adept at communicating with plant spirits in a certain way. When you acquire the ability, cultivate it by practicing it. That does not mean that you forget about the other ways of communication. You should focus on them all but definitely play to your strengths.

A great way to hone your skills is to practice the meditation walk described in the previous chapter. Walk around in nature and be mindful of everything around you. The more you interact with nature, the more you will be drawn to certain plants or nature spirits. You will often find that you connect with a spirit or are drawn to it when you are not thinking about it. Be mindful and purposeful about connecting with nature, but don't necessarily look for the spirit energy.

Listen for the spirits when you are out in nature. As previously mentioned, trees are powerful in Druidry, and you will find a lot of plant spirit energy in trees, especially in the roots that dive deep into the ground. Keep practicing your nature walks and meditation and mindfulness, and you will find the spirits.

One other thing to keep in mind, and it can be funny to think about, is that the spirits of nature are just like you or me. You will not commune with a spirit and find the answers to the universe. You might only get a feeling from them, a problem you can help with, or they might just tell you that they are thirsty. The message or intention you get from a plant spirit might also come to you over an extended period, so do not expect an answer or messages instantly. And, as the seasons change, the spirits change too. Some plant spirits are only around at certain times of the year, while others might lie dormant for a season.

When you do find yourself drawn to a plant, tree, or another nature spirit, use these steps to create more of a connection:

1. First, choose your plant. You might find yourself drawn to a special plant as you walk around in nature, interacting with the plants and trees.
2. Be with the plant. This is going to be a relationship, so be with the plant when you are in nature. This is as simple as sitting with a plant or tree. You could sit in a tree if you want or give it a hug.
3. Open yourself up to the plant spirit. Try to feel what the plant is feeling. Does the plant spirit want you there? Remember, this is not just about you. Are they happy or sad? Can you feel a message or intention?
4. You can make an offering if you feel you have a bond with the plant spirit. Tobacco and sage are good offerings; you can also sing to the plant or play an instrument.
5. Care for the plant if it needs it. If the plant is fine, you can just be with it. If it needs help, you can strengthen your bond by watering or feeding it.

When you open yourself up to a plant spirit, you need to be ready to accept the message in any way it comes. You might get a simple message from the plant that will be easy to interpret. But the message might also be cryptic, and you might need to meditate on it. Ancestor meditation might help you find the answer. You might also get a feeling, an image, a word, or a song. It could be a melody, an unknown language, or energy. Be receptive to what is given to you, and do not worry if you cannot figure out the meaning immediately. Usually, the message you get will be something that can help you. So, if you are seeking answers in your life, be sure to ask the nature spirits and then interpret what they are telling you.

Spirit Animals

Most people in life have a spirit animal that helps guide them through life. The problem is that few people know what the spirit animal is or how they can use the power of their spirit animal. You first need to know what your spirit animal is, and then you need to foster a relationship so you can unlock the power of your animal companion.

It's important to connect with your spirit animal.
https://pixabay.com/es/photos/lobos-wolf-pack-bosque-animales-2864647/

You might already know your spirit animal. Have you felt drawn to a specific animal? Have you felt an animal has been trying to communicate with you? Do you feel something inside but don't know what the feeling is? All of these questions might be pointing to your spirit animal ally. Your spirit animal is both something internal and external. They are there in times of need, but we do not often recognize them or accept their help. By unlocking your animal ally, you are unblocking your path through life.

There are a few ways you can discover your spirit animal; one of those ways is - yes, meditation! Although, this can be a tricky one as animal spirit guides can help us with meditation and journeying. You might be able to meet your animal spirit by doing the same journey meditation as you did in ancestral meditation, but it can be difficult. A better method is visualization. Meditate and try to visualize your spirit animal. This can be made easier by trying the following two methods first, Being Present and Dreaming.

You have taken many walks in nature, and you have been mindful of those walks. What have you found? Do you find the same animal coming to you again and again? When you pay attention in life, do you notice animals popping up in your day-to-day life? Are they in songs, books, or movies? Be mindful as you go about your day, and keep in mind the animals that show up far too much to be a coincidence. The same is true with dreams. When you dream, are you always dreaming of the same animal? Be intentional when going to sleep. State your intent before you fall asleep: *"I want my spirit animal to visit me in my dream."*

The more you think about your spirit animal, the more you are going to find it in your life. And, when you know your spirit animal, you can journey through meditation and visit them. Learn more about your spirit animal. Dogs are known to be loyal, hawks have great eyesight, and elephants have amazing memories. The better you know your spirit animal, the better you will know yourself, and you can foster a better connection by using your knowledge of your spirit guide to better react to events in your life. You will also find that visiting the astral plane (which we will talk about more in the next chapter, is easier when you have unblocked your own path, and your animal spirit will walk by your side when you leave the mortal plane.

The Fae

The fae encompasses many different beings. Fae and fairy sound very similar, and there is a connection there. Many different beings belong to the fae, including elves, minor deities, elementals, nature spirits, shapeshifters, and more. They inhabit a world that is between our human world and the world of the gods and goddesses. Because of this, they can have more influence on the human world, and they can shape our lives.

The ancient Druids were much more in tune with the fae-folk, so some work has to be done to reconnect with them. As a species, we have been living our lives far from the fae, and that has given them a reason to live far from us. By being intentional and searching them out, we can be better prepared both in life and when we travel the astral plane. The fae is experts on the astral plane, so we should search them out as guides.

The fae might be separate from our world, but they are still deeply connected to nature. As you immerse yourself in nature, you naturally place yourself closer to the fae. Ancient Druids were more in touch with the fae because they were more in touch with their spiritual selves. You can become more in touch with your spiritual self by communing with your ancestors and finding your spirit animal. The more you work on your spirit, the more the fae will be attracted to you.

When you are looking to connect with the fae in nature, continue to meditate and be mindful, but state your intention as you walk through the woods or by a river: "I invite the fairies and elves to walk with me today." Continue to repeat your intent as you walk.

You can also create an altar for the fae-folk. You can set up an altar as you did for your ancestors, both indoors and out in nature, but instead of personal artifacts, you can give offerings. Milk and honey are both excellent offerings for the fae-folk. They are attracted to sweet things, so you can bake something and place that on your altar too. Fruit, herbs, spices, and sugar can also be used. Instead of an altar outside, you can also create a fairy garden.

Once you have your altar, spend time there, just as you would spend time with your ancestors. Remember that you are communing with beings from another world, so this will take time. You might not get anything straight away, but do not give up or lose hope. Keep practicing, and they will come to you; they will see your intentions.

You can meditate at your altar and try meditation or journeying to better communicate with the spirits. They live on the astral plane, and if you can journey to where they are, you can have a better relationship. Fae-folk will sometimes visit our plane, but you will have better luck if you visit them. Practice visiting and communing with them; when you meet them on the astral plane, they will be more welcoming and more ready to help guide you on your astral journeys.

Chapter 5: Moving to the Otherworld

You might have started on your journey into Hedge Druidry because you had heard about astral projection. In the previous chapter, we touched on the journey slightly. When you do ancestor meditation, you often travel into the astral plane. This is an excellent place to start, as your ancestors are there to welcome and help you. There is a place for you to go, a destination, which makes the process much easier. As we mentioned in that chapter, any form of Druid meditation can give no results the first few times, so it is a skill you will need to be proactive and hone.

Moving through to the other world is even harder, and there is no point in trying it until you have mastered some other skills. By preparing first, you will have a better chance of success. Before you even think about traveling to the astral plane, you should focus on being in nature, creating an altar or shrine, convening with the spirits, ancestor meditation, and visualization. You should also unlock your spirit animal. Druidry is a process and not something that you can dip your toes into every aspect of all at once.

And, if you are going to travel into the other world, you are going to need some guides. Your body will not become lost, but if you lose your way or get yourself in any danger, it will affect your mind and soul. So, before you travel to the other world, you should be on good terms with the nature spirits and fae folk. You should also have unlocked your spirit animal to help guide you, and you will need to have convened with your ancestors and visited them. And do not just take my word for it. If you are trying to decide whether you are ready or not, you can ask that question of your ancestors. They are experts in the other world and will know when your time is right.

Having all those spirits and nature on your side will make it easier for you to travel to the astral plane and navigate when you are there. And the point of this travel is to gather more insight into the world and ask spiritual questions. How would you like it if someone turned up at your house and you had no idea who they were? You might invite them in and give them some food, Druids are very welcoming, but you would not share any personal information with them. Get to know the beings and spirits you visit before going there.

Because you might be deeply affected by the process of astral travel, you'll need to learn how to ground yourself before and after you travel. This will bring your mind back to the physical world and help you to know you have returned to the physical world. When you are starting out on your astral plane journey, it is always recommended that you start small. Work on everything we've discussed so far in this book, work on it for a long time, and then try astral travel. Some people can never do it, but if you are diligent in your preparation and practice a lot, it should become open to you.

Grounding before and after Astral Travel

Grounding is important, and not just for astral travel. When we use the word grounding, we could substitute it with "mindfulness." By being mindful when you are out in nature, you are grounding yourself in this world. You feel more a part of this world, and that is beneficial in many ways. Not only are you noticing the world around you and taking it in, but you are reminding yourself that this is the world you live in; this is your home.

Grounding might not seem an important thing when you are walking through this world to remind yourself that you are in this world, but it is a good practice to get into when you want to continue your development within the astral plane. And mindfulness is going to help you to meditate in nature more freely, further honing your skills. All this to say, everything is connected. When you practice one skill, it cascades into the next.

When you are planning astral travel, it is important to practice grounding before you attempt it. You can do this when in nature or use some of the techniques you will be shown below. Grounding should be done before you travel to give you a starting point, and it should be done after you travel to bring an end to the travel. And we only need to look at the effects of PTSD or flashbacks to understand the importance of grounding.

People with PTSD and other afflictions relive traumatic memories. They get caught up in their minds, and it has been shown that grounding helps to combat that. While astral projection seems like an amazing thing (and it is), you are traveling to a world you know nothing about, and the things you might experience there can be beyond your understanding. When your mind cannot comprehend something, it can take a toll. So, not only is grounding and mindfulness an excellent thing to practice around astral travel, but it is good to practice during your day when you start astral projection. If you are already practicing mindfulness, you are already in the habit.

So, along with being mindful of nature, what can you specifically do to ground yourself before and after traveling to the other world?

- Simply say your name and a little bit about yourself. That helps to bring your mind back to the present. "My name is John Smith, I live in Edinburgh, and I had toast for breakfast this morning." Saying this out loud might sound silly, but it is an extremely effective grounding technique to distract your mind.
- Breathe deeply. Take ten breaths in and out, focusing on each one and counting each one. You can do this with your eyes closed before and after you travel, or you can focus on a single point in your room or in nature to focus your mind.
- Use water. One method is to drink cold water, slowly sipping it and feeling the coolness in your mouth and in your throat and stomach. Remember, water also helps to focus your psychic energy. Or you can wash your hands and face in cold water, focusing on the sensation as you do. You do not even need to use water. You can have an ice pack or something else cold on hand to press to your forehead or neck. Not only is the sensation calming, but you can be mindful of the feeling too.
- Soothe yourself. Before you go into the astral plane and after you come out of it, tell yourself where you are. You can go as far as to talk about your country, city, address, and room. This helps your mind leave the astral plane and return to the physical plane.

- With your eyes still closed, you can focus on what your body feels. Are your clothes tight or loose? Do they rub against you? Are you cold or warm? Is your behind numb from sitting on the floor?
- Use sound. If you are in nature, you can listen to the sounds you hear around you. Can you hear the birds chirping, the wind blowing, the stream babbling? If you are indoors, you can do the same, but if you are in a quiet room, you can play some music or nature sounds and focus on them when you return.
- Look around you and be mindful. When you are back in the physical world, things look different. Find different colors around you, look for the light shining off things in different ways, and find textures and shapes.
- Use an elastic band. Place an elastic band around your wrist, and when you are back from the astral plane, flick the elastic against your skin gently, concentrating on the feeling.
- This is not an exhaustive list, and from reading it, you should have an idea of the types of things that you can do to ground yourself before and after traveling. Find what works for you if nothing on this list is appealing.

Practice grounding each day to feel more connected to the physical world, and the more you practice, the easier it will be when it comes time to travel. Grounding will help to protect your mind, and it helps you to distinguish between the two worlds by becoming more connected to this one.

Traveling to the Astral Plane

Not to put you off before you travel to the astral plane, but there are certain things you should do before going there. The first is grounding, and the second is to create some wards. Wards are basically magic spells that will protect you while you travel. When you think about it, astral traveling means you are splitting your body in half. Your body stays in this world, and your mind goes to the next. You might face some dangers there. This isn't to put you off traveling; it's only being discussed to help you to travel by knowing what is waiting for you. For example, if you are learning to ride a bike, you start with your feet on the ground (grounding), and you know there is a chance of falling off and injuring yourself, so you wear a helmet (wards). You know the dangers, but you still ride your bike. The same is true for astral travel.

Using Wards before Astral Travel

So, you are off traveling to the astral plane. Your body is in a room back in your home, and you might even have locked your door. You are pretty safe, right? You are if you take precautions. You are starting on your journey into astral travel, so it makes sense that there are other beings out there who can travel between worlds. In fact, many spirits can travel between the other world and the physical world quite easily. That spirit could very easily enter your body and make a home, living as a kind of parasitic entity that drains your psychic energy.

You could also pick up some bad energy on your travels. The spirit world is much like ours, and just as you might pick up a bad hitchhiker on your travels, you can have a bad spirit or energy attach itself to your mind and spirit as you journey. You might even have some of your spirit and energy sucked into the astral world, and you go back feeling drained and maybe not able to travel again.

Wards can protect against all of this. They protect your body when your mind is away from it, they stop your spirit from being drawn into the spirit world without your permission, and they stop negative energies from returning with your mind.

I am going to teach you two common defensive wards to protect you when you are in the other world. There are many more spells and wards to learn for astral travel, both offensive and defensive, and once you start out, you will want to research more about what you can do, but that is beyond the scope of this book. We are going to start small and take the first step on your journey, and you can go from there.

Ward Spell

What you will need: writing implements, paper, rosemary, lavender, basil, quartz crystals, and some small envelopes.

1. Write your intent on the paper: *"This ward is to stop negative energy from entering my physical body while I travel and to protect my mind."* As you start to travel more, you might change the wording based on where you go and what you see. Create four copies of this same ward.

2. Place each piece of paper in its own envelope and add the herbs and crystals to the envelopes too.
3. Seal the envelopes.
4. Place the envelopes around you, either in the corners of the room you are in or facing the four cardinal directions.

Glyph Ward

Instead of using four envelopes with ingredients inside, you can use four glyphs. The glyph we are going to use is the glyph for luck. It consists of three interlocking circles. Simply draw the glyphs on pieces of paper and place them around you. Alternatively, you can draw them on rocks and place them around you for protection.

Your First Astral Steps

While it is possible for spontaneous astral travel to happen or astral travel to happen in dreams (lucid dreaming), we are going to explore intentional astral walking, also known as an out-of-body experience (OBE). There is a lot you need to know, and we will break it down into numbered steps that contain a lot of information, but it is important to know everything before you begin. We'll start with astral walking close to your body and then instruct you on how that can transfer to walking the other world with your ancestors or spirit animal.

1. Choose a place from which to travel. You want this to be somewhere familiar, so it is not a shock when you leave your body. You also want to find a place where you will not be disturbed. If your body is disturbed, your mind will snap back to your body, and that can be a shock to the system. You either want to be sitting or lying down. And you want to be wearing comfortable clothing. Any discomfort is going to make it harder for you to travel.

2. Before you get comfortable, set up either one or both of the wards outlined above. You may have traveled to the astral plane many times and never needed the wards, but just like wearing a helmet when you are riding a bike, you do not need it until you do.

3. Sit or lie down and perform one of the grounding exercises detailed above. It is important that you perform the same grounding exercise both at the start and the end of the travel.

4. Close your eyes and try to relax. If you have been practicing your ancestral meditation and nature meditation, you should find this easy. Try to clear your mind of all thoughts and concentrate only on your breathing. Let the tension flow from your body. Do not worry if you find your mind wandering; simply bring it back to your breathing each time. The more you practice, the easier this will get. Do not even think about your spirit leaving your body; just let it happen naturally. If you are still finding it hard, you can hold a quartz crystal in your hand and feel the vibrations running through your body.

5. Your mind will eventually reach a state where it feels as if you are falling asleep. This is the hardest part of astral traveling. You are not falling asleep, though if you let yourself relax more, your body will fall asleep. Your mind is trying to leave the body, and this is what shuts the body down. You need your body to sleep but your mind to stay alert. Instead of pushing your mind from your body, let it wander your body. Feel your body start to sleep. Be aware of each body part, one at a time, and feel it start to rest. Feel as it becomes separate from you. In this state, you want to think about it as your body being removed from your mind and not your mind leaving your body.

6. In your mind, move each part of your body. Start with your fingers and toes. Visualize then curling and uncurling. If you find your body reacting, go back and try to find the liminal state between waking and sleeping. Keep visualizing your body moving in your mind even though it is not physically moving. Move around your entire body, visualizing it moving as you stay in this liminal state.

7. It is at this point that you might feel energy running through your body, perhaps a vibration. Embrace that. If you feel this energy, then you know that you are doing it right. Do not become excited by it, or you risk triggering your body. Simply be aware of it and accept it.

8. When you feel ready, remove your mind from your body. You should be able to visualize the room you are in. Stand up and look down on your body in its mediative/hypnotic state. It's recommended at this point that you move back into your body on your first attempt, then go through the grounding in the last steps. You want to take it one step at a time to become accustomed to it,

and you know you can now do it. After a few practice runs, you can move on to the next steps.

9. When you are able to separate your mind from your body, you can start to travel. But, before then, it is a good idea to confirm that you are actually traveling and not visualizing. Move around the room and look for something that you have not really noticed before. Study it, taking in the shape, color, etc. When you return to your body and wake up, you can search out the item and see if you traveled when you were meditating.

10. When you leave your body, do not look back at it. This act helps you to venture further. Move out of the room or area you are in, passing through the door if you need to. You will not be able to interact with objects when you are on the astral plane.

11. A good place to visit on the astral plane is the parts of nature you have been walking. When you are there, you might see some plant and nature spirits if they are open to accepting you. If you have been communing with the plant spirits, this is more likely to happen. You might see your spirit animal ally while you travel. You might even see some of the fae-folk or other spirits that are astral traveling. Feel free to interact with them if they are open to interacting with you.

12. Go as far as you are comfortable with, and when you are ready, you can return to your body, stepping back into it. Take a moment after this to gently wake your body by thinking about each part of your body and slowly moving it.

13. Repeat the grounding exercise that you performed before traveling. Take some time after to process what you just did. When you feel you are fully in control of your body, you can go about your day.

Astral Traveling Tips

- Always keep a notebook by your side after you have traveled. The longer you leave it after traveling, the more you will forget, so journal your experience as soon as you are done traveling so you can be intentional with each journey that comes after.

- When you start seeing your animal spirit companion and the other nature or fae spirits, you can interact with them. This is a good time to prepare questions and problems that they might be able to help with or questions about life and the universe. The spirits know more than we do, and, for the most part, they want to share with us.

- Look for a guide. Your spirit animal is a part of you, but it also resides in the astral plane. When you travel there and interact with your spirit animal, follow it or ask it to lead you places. This is the safest guide you will have on your astral travel. You can also look to nature and fae spirits to guide you. Be receptive to them, and do not question where they take you but why they take you. You might see things that you do not want to see, but the goal is for you to see what you need to see.

- When you become more adept at astral travel, use it to travel to and with your ancestors. You will have already practiced ancestor meditation, and this is traveling in the astral plane, but it is different from astral travel. When you reach your meditative state, look for an entrance to the sea realm, or ask your spirit animal or one of the other spirits. When you reach your ancestors, you will have more interaction with them, and they will also be able to show you places. Of course, this is only going to work if you already have a relationship with them.

Astral projection is not something that everyone will do as a Druid, and if you do travel the astral realm, it will likely take a lot of time to learn. There are some people who spend years learning to astral travel, and my best tip is to go back to what you learned in earlier chapters and practice them a lot. Be in nature, be mindful, practice meditation, and be careful and deliberate when it does come time to travel the astral plane.

When you are able to travel the astral plane, you will find a lot of worth in being able to do it. Not only is it a liberating experience, but you can also find answers there that you cannot find in the physical world. As a Hedge Druid, you are also going to find a community there with other beings that have similar values. Of course, you will also find some that do not share anything in common with you, and that is valuable in itself.

Practice the basics, and then move on to astral travel. Who knows, we might even see each other there.

Chapter 6: Sacred Herbs, Plants, and Trees

You will find out later that trees are very important in Druidry, and there is an entire alphabet dedicated to trees, with a different tree representing a letter of the alphabet. You will already have spent a lot of time in nature, and that will give you a chance to see the herbs, plants, and trees around you, but you should always strive to know more. We'll consider some common Druid uses for some sacred plants and herbs, but you should always do your own research before you go out and pick plants for use. And you should always remember to take what can be given and thank nature for what it gives.

Another thing to do is to create your own grimoire in which you write down the plants and herbs you use, where you found them, what they looked like, how they tasted, and the effect they had. You can use your grimoire to plant your own garden outside – or inside your home if you don't have a garden. You can then add to your grimoire as you tend to your plants and herbs over the years.

You might also notice that some plants and herbs open you up more to the Awen. We'll discuss some uses later in this chapter, but plants and herbs will affect people differently, so if you feel an effect that attaches you better to the Awen, the spiritual world, or helps you to meditate, etc., you should write that down and try to incorporate that into your practices.

Herbs and plants are used by Druids.
https://www.pexels.com/photo/person-holding-black-scissors-3912947/

Common Druids Herbs and Plants and Their Uses

This is not a comprehensive list by any means, and you should do further research into plants, herbs, and trees, especially those in your area. Being a Druid is about working with nature, and there is no subset of nature that is for Druids only. To be a Druid, you need to learn about all of the plants and herbs out there.

Wheat

Used to demote the harvest and a crop that can be used to decorate your dwelling or eaten in food around the Autumn Equinox.

Beans

Deep associations with the underworld and death. When celebrating with your ancestors, you can offer beans to them at the ancestral altar, and you can include beans in your foods.

Burdock, Birch Sap, and Dandelion

All three can be boiled up and distilled into elixirs than can be drunk to boost health, so include some as part of your diet and add more when you are not feeling well. They can also help with connecting to the astral plane, so drink any of the three before attempting astral travel or meditation.

Mugwort

Mugwort can be made into tea, and it has been said that it can induce altered consciousness. This aids with journeying, so if you are having trouble entering the spiritual world or traveling from your body, try some mugwort tea before you practice.

Primrose and Vervain

If you brew and distill either or both, you can create a tincture that can be used to bless. Create an infusion and sprinkle it over your altar.

Cloves and Garlic

Both help to ward off evil spirits, and if you are traveling or welcoming spirits or ancestors into your home, you can leave cloves of garlic at the threshold of your rooms to stop unwanted spirits from crossing over.

Juniper Berries

Turn them into a perfume that can be applied to the body or sprayed into a room to cleanse your aura or your space.

Agrimony

Make soap with agrimony in it so you can dispel sorrow when you are washing. The plant is known to draw out negative energy. If you do not want to make soap with the plant, you can wash the plant over your face and body instead to help cleanse.

Fern

When you become more adept at Druid magic, you can use ferns to create invisibility. Until then, you can carry some fern with you to help you not stand out and blend in more in a crowd. If you need to pass unnoticed, the fern will help.

Mandrake

Dry the plant and include it in a necklace, locket, or a small bag you can carry. Mandrake helps to clear out your aura and create a general sense of well-being and happiness.

Yarrow

If you find that you are having problems with divination, try making divination sticks from yarrow or having some yarrow close to you when you are practicing.

Meadowsweet

Use when brewing mead and drink the mead to help with an upset stomach. You can also place some in your bath to help with a fever or aches.

Raspberry

Eat the berries and brew the leaves into tea. The tea can be a painkiller for those who are in labor, and a stronger brew of the tea can help with an upset stomach.

Chamomile

You probably know this plant as a tea. You can find some in the wild and brew up your own tea after drying the flowers. It can be used to help calm your body and help you get to sleep. It is also beneficial for digestion and aids with upset and sore stomachs.

Cowslip

The plant can be distilled into wine, or you can add the flowers into a recipe for any skin cream. Use after being in the sun to soothe the skin and treat rashes. You can apply it to sore joints to soothe inflammation and stiffness, and the wine can be consumed for the same ailment. Brew up the root into a tincture that can soothe a sore throat.

Dandelion

The stem and flowers can be eaten, and the roots can be roasted and brewed into coffee. Dandelion helps to cleanse the body and release toxins, improving liver function.

As with any new food that you add to a diet, especially one you will be picking and processing yourself, it is essential that you do thorough research before you consume any of them. The plants and herbs on this list are not dangerous if consumed in the right way and in moderation, but you should investigate each one and build your knowledge first before you eat or drink any of them.

If you have any health conditions, you should consult with your doctor before you add any of these to your diet. The herbs and plants on the list are safe to eat, but improve your knowledge and wisdom first and ensure you know nature before you use it.

Chapter 7: Reading the Tree Alphabet

Many older languages started as simple markings that might resemble the letters we have in our alphabet today, but many of them did not have the curved lines and cursive writing that our letters have. You will find that many of the older languages relied on straight lines that were easy to carve into trees and rocks with simple tools.

We can easily differentiate between modern letters and runes, and you might already picture shapes in your head when you think about runes. The tree alphabet, also known as ogham letters, is made up of straight lines, mostly vertical and horizontal, joined and crossing lines. There are twenty main letters, and each letter corresponds to a tree hence, the tree alphabet. This link is most likely down to two things, the strong link between paganism and nature and the fact that the lines resemble trees, with one main line standing vertically and the other lines branching off from it.

The History of the Tree Alphabet

It is hard to pinpoint exactly when the tree alphabet was first used. There are definitely inscriptions that have been found carved into trees, tools, rocks, and other surfaces that date back to as early as the 5th century, but some scholars suggest that the alphabet goes back farther than that. As with any historical writings and artifacts, etc., we can only date them as far back as they were discovered to be used, but it is almost certain that they predate that time and have just not been discovered in that time yet, or the evidence has been lost.

There were many other languages around during the time of the Druids, and one theory put forward for the creation of the tree alphabet is that it was to be used as a form of code. Druids and other pagans could use the alphabet to communicate in secret at a time when they needed to. This was also a time when invasions were common, and war was always a possibility. Just like the codes that were created during the World Wars, the tree alphabet could have been used to send secret messages on the battlefield without the enemy uncovering plans and tactics.

Those are the modern interpretations of the history of the tree alphabet, but as discussed above, likely, the ogham letters were already around before they needed to be used as code, so there is also a possibility that they were created differently. In folklore and in some religions, there is the story of the tower of babel. Humankind, in their infinite wisdom, tried to build a tower to heaven. This was back when there was no modern machinery like cranes. They would not have reached the heavens, but the gods decided to punish humankind for their ignorance and dispersed the people, giving them all different languages so they could not speak to each other and coordinate such an effort again.

A scholar traveled to the failed tower soon after to find that all of the languages of the world had been given out, and there were none left to take. He spent years studying the languages and took the best of each one, creating a language all of his own. From that language, he created a few extensions, and one of those became the tree alphabet.

Whichever method of creation you favor, the letters are here, and they are available for you to use. But you need to be careful with them. It is true that words have power, but that is even truer with the tree alphabet. You need to be careful with their use, and the letters can often be used in spells and divination, which we will talk about in the next chapter, so be sure that you know how to use them before you start to write with them.

The Ogham Letters

The Ogham alphabet is split up into twenty letters. There are more symbols that can be used in divination, but let's talk about them in the next chapter. Within the alphabet, we can better split the letters into four sub-categories. Each letter in the alphabet has a vertical line, and there is a combination of horizontal lines. The horizontal lines are either on the

Right, Left, Diagonal, or Through. Let us take a look at each section one by one.

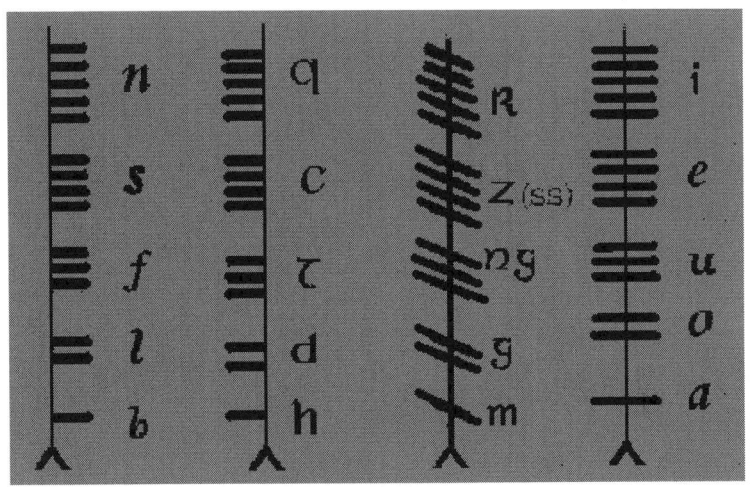

Ogham alphabet.
The original uploader was Anárion at English Wikipedia., CC BY 1.0 <https://creativecommons.org/licenses/by/1.0>, via Wikimedia Commons https://commons.wikimedia.org/wiki/File:Oghamalfabet.gif

I will also give you the magical focus for each ogham letter that you can use when performing ogham divination, which will be detailed in the next chapter.

Right (Horizontal Lines Starting at the Vertical Line and Running to the Right)

B (Beith)

Tree: Birch

Description: Vertical line with one horizontal line to the right.

Meaning: This is the letter of new beginnings, change, and rebirth. It can also mean a spiritual rebirth, a cleansing of the soul. Birch is a strong and hardy tree that can grow almost anywhere, and the wood and bark are often used in hard furniture and tools.

Magical Focus: Get rid of the negative, look for change, and be grateful. Look for the positive, renew and rebirth, and fill the emptiness.

L (Luis)

Tree: Rowan

Description: Vertical line with two horizontal lines to the right.

Meaning: This is the letter of protection and safety. Rowan trees are often used in protection rituals and spells, and you might also notice that if you split the berry of the rowan tree, the inside looks similar to a pentagram, adding more magic to this letter.

Magical Focus: Protection, looks for wisdom and insight, follow your intuition, be aware of your surroundings, look for that which means to harm you, and remain grounded.

F (Fearn)

Tree: Alder

Description: Vertical line with three horizontal lines to the right.

Meaning: This letter denotes the month of March and is strongly connected to the Spring Equinox. It can also be used to symbolize a bridge, both physical and magical. Alders grow in swamp regions where other trees would not, meaning it is a hardy tree.

Magical Focus: Survival where others cannot build bridges, knowing who you are, finding uniqueness in others, mending what is broken, giving advice.

S (Saille)

Tree: Willow

Description: Vertical line with four horizontal lines to the right.

Meaning: This is the letter of water as willows are often found growing close to a source of an abundance of water. Not only does this letter denote physical growth, but it promotes spiritual growth too. It is a symbol often used in protection rituals.

Magical Focus: Protection, femininity, healing, growth, going on a journey, being ready, go with the flow.

N (Nion)

Tree: Ash

Description: Vertical line with five horizontal lines to the right.

Meaning: Ash trees are one of the most sacred trees in Druid circles, and this makes the letter one of the most powerful. You can look to this letter as a link between the worlds.

Magical Focus: being responsible for your actions, connection, bringing people together, thinking about your words, and considering nature.

Left (Horizontal Lines Starting at the Vertical Line and Running to the Left)

H (Huath)

Tree: Hawthorn

Description: Vertical line with one horizontal line to the left.

Meaning: Hawthorns are usually prickly and are used for protection in rituals and spells. You can also write the letter on jewelry to wear to give yourself extra protection, and the letter is great when you are performing astral projection. The letter is also associated with fae-folk.

Magical Focus: Offer protection, communicate with the spirits, aid in fertility, look to help others, and find spiritual strength.

D (Duir)

Tree: Oak

Description: Vertical line with two horizontal lines to the left.

Meaning: This letter is mighty, just like the tree it symbolizes. You can consider this the king of the letters, presiding over all the others. The letter is associated with masculinity and protection.

Magical Focus: Aid in fertility, masculinity, offer protection, be a leader, luck, look for the unexpected, find opportunity, and be resilient.

T (Tinne)

Tree: Holly

Description: Vertical line with three horizontal lines to the left.

Meaning: Holly was often used to craft weapons, and the letter is a letter of power. It is another protective letter that can be used in the astral plane and can be used to ward off negative spirits.

Magical Focus: The seasons are changing, rebirth, offer protection for the family, fight back, be honorable, and stand with those around you.

C (Coll)

Tree: Hazel

Description: Vertical line with four horizontal lines to the left.

Meaning: This letter is the life force of the alphabet, just like the hazel tree gifts hazelnuts. Usually, hazel trees were found near sacred waters, so you can use the letter to symbolize that too. It is a powerful letter in divination.

Magical Focus: Find what is sacred, wisdom, aid in creativity, lead those around you, commune with the spirit world, and find a muse.

Q (Quert)

Tree: Apple

Description: Vertical line with five horizontal lines to the left.

Meaning: Apples can mean a realization or a giving of knowledge, perhaps a total rebirth, just like with the apple of Eden. Red apples are also associated with nourishment and love.

Magical Focus: Blossoming love, the harvest, tackling difficult choices, knowing how-to guide, choosing your path, interpreting the signs.

Diagonal (Horizontal Lines Passing through the Vertical Line on a Diagonal)

M (Muin)

Tree: Vine

Description: Vertical line with one horizontal line passing through on a diagonal.

Meaning: This is a letter of truth. Just as wine might make us speak without thinking about it, often the truth, the letter can invoke that too. You can use it to find the truth, and placing it around your person, will help you to be more truthful both to yourself and others.

Magical Focus: Look for the truth, tell the truth, and be introspective. Think before you speak, look to the future, and think about things.

G (Got)

Tree: Ivy

Description: Vertical line with two horizontal lines passing through on a diagonal.

Meaning: Vines spiral around trellises and trees and bushes, usually upward towards the sun. We can use this letter to represent our spiritual growth as we go around in circles but always move upward. This letter can also be used to denote death. A vine will still live even after what it was growing on has died, just as our spirit will live on.

Magical Focus: Growth, life after death, look for positive relationships, remove negativity, look inside, and grow, ask for help, and find community.

nG (nGeatal)

Tree: Reed

Description: Vertical line with three horizontal lines passing through on a diagonal.

Meaning: It can represent both music and battle as reeds were often used to fashion both arrows, flutes, and other musical instruments). Both end products are about action, so use this letter as a letter of action or to help inspire you to action.

Magical Focus: A call to action, be with family and friends, heal, be a leader, rebuild what is broken, find order, spiritual journeys, and understanding.

St (Straith)

Tree: Blackthorn

Description: Vertical line with four horizontal lines passing through on a diagonal.

Meaning: The blackthorn tree was long associated with winning, often flown on banners or prayed under after winning a battle. It is also a tree where the berries come after the first frost, making it a symbol of nourishment when there is little left.

Magical Focus: Facing adversity, tackling problems head-on, looking for the unexpected, surprising, overcoming obstacles, and making changes.

R (Ruis)

Tree: Elder

Description: Vertical line with five horizontal lines passing through on a diagonal.

Meaning: this letter is often used around the Winter Solstice. You can add this letter to celebrations near the end of the year when things are coming to an end. But it is also a letter of rebirth. What once was ended will be reborn again, and the great cycle of life goes on.

Magical Focus: Physical and spiritual rebirth, endings, new beginnings, gaining wisdom and knowledge, feeling like a child again, continuing to grow.

Through (Horizontal Lines Passing Straight Through the Vertical Line)

A (Ailm)

Tree: Elm

Description: Vertical line with one straight horizontal line passing through.

Meaning: The elm tree is a tall tree, often towering over the other trees in a forest, and this letter represents the statuesque nature of the meaning. You can use this letter when you want to convey clear sight. Just as the elm can tower above and see what has come and what is to come, so can you see better when utilizing this letter.

Magical Focus: Find meaning in the past, look to the future, be flexible, grow spiritually, find wisdom, allow others to follow, and become a leader.

O (Onn)

Tree: Gorse

Description: Vertical line with two straight horizontal lines passing through.

Meaning: This letter is a source of nourishment, both physically and spiritually. The gorse bush would give food for people and animals, and entire ecosystems would grow around it. Gorse bushes thrive when they are burned down to make way for new growth, and we can apply this to our life. When we get rid of the old, we have room for what is new.

Magical Focus: Get rid of the deadwood, find growth, and protection, follow your dreams, go on a journey, and mentor another.

U (Uhr)

Tree: Heather

Description: Vertical line with three straight horizontal lines passing through.

Meaning: Heather is an attractive plant, and, just as heather would provide pollen for bees, the letter can be used to denote beauty or the gifting of beauty. You can use the letter to better promote healing or give off any kind, both physically and spiritually.

Magical Focus: Give a gift, heal, look for beauty, let go of stress, listen to your body, focus on your spirit, and time to meditate.

E (Eadhadh)

Tree: Aspen

Description: Vertical line with four straight horizontal lines passing through.

Meaning: A durable and hardy tree that can grow almost anywhere. This letter is a hardy one that can be combined with others to boost and strengthen them. It is a letter of success and conquering. Many heroes in mythology and folklore and shown with this symbol.

Magical Focus: Look to the fae-folk, be flexible, let go of your worries, be brave, open yourself to experiences, forget material possessions, and take a journey.

I (Ioadhadh)

Tree: Yew

Description: Vertical line with five straight horizontal lines passing through.

Meaning: The yew represents death, and this can be seen as the letter of death, but do not worry, in Druid circles, the notion of death is simply a transition or change. Even when we physically die, our spirit lives on.

Magical Focus: Rebirth, new life, transitions, and change, minimize your life, welcome what is to come, look for obstacles, and accept your fear.

Writing with the Ogham Letters

That is all there is to the letters in the main alphabet. The letters can have power if you use them in certain rituals and spells, but if you stick to just writing the letters to record though and feelings, you will be fine. Just be mindful that when you are writing the letter, you are conveying something. So, while writing letters in a journal to record your emotions while in the astral plane might do just that, carving ogham letters into a tree might have an unintended effect.

You will notice that each letter in the alphabet has something in common. Each has a vertical line. This makes it easy to write long sequences of letters. You can draw a straight line down the side of your page and then add the branching lines to denote letters, leaving gaps for spaces. With a little practice, writing and reading like this can become second nature. As we are a society that usually writes from left to right, from the top of the page to the bottom, you can also turn the letters on their side. You can instead draw a horizontal line across your page and then add branching vertical lines that represent each letter turned onto its side.

It takes a little practice to memorize all of the letters and write them freely, but at least there is no cursive to practice. The great thing about the letters is you are going to be able to write them easily, and they are going to be easy to read, no matter how bad your handwriting usually is! And they are grouped by their horizontal lines. It is much easier to learn them in groups like this rather than trying to memorize the letters in alphabetical order.

So, what can you do with the alphabet?

In the next chapter, we'll see how to perform divination with them, but for now, we only need to concern ourselves with basic writing and some basic rune use.

As already mentioned, you can use the Ogham letters as a regular alphabet and use them to write in journals or books. They are not as quick as using the regular alphabet, so you might want to use the letters to record private thoughts and feelings that you do not want anyone else to see.

The letters have power, so do not be fooled into using them to decorate, as they can have unintended consequences. You can, however, use them as runes. Use the letters individually, and use them to represent a specific intent. For example, when you are traveling to the astral plane, and you want to protect your physical body, you can choose one of the letters than denotes protection and draw it on four pieces of paper to leave around you. You have created a rune that is going to help protect.

You can do the same with any of the letters. For example, if you need more confidence or luck, you might carve the duir into a necklace and wear it around your neck. You can see from the descriptions above what each of the letters means, and you can choose them accordingly. Just make sure that you only use one letter at a time. By doing so, you know the intent you are creating. When you start to combine letters into runes, you might create unintended intents.

Chapter 8: Ogham Divination

You can use the letters laid out in the previous chapter to perform ogham divination. This basically means that you are using the letters to see into the future, seeing events, what might happen, and things to come, or gain insight or knowledge of the world around you.

Like many things in the Druid world, you will need to practice. Doing the actual divination part is easy. You might select a few letters at random, and you are done. But you need to interpret the letters. If you draw the letter for luck, does this mean that good luck is coming your way or bad luck? If you draw multiple protection runes, do you need protection, should you protect someone else, or are you gifted protection?

With ogham divination, the more you perform it, the better you will get at it, and when you are interpreting the results, you need to think about what you find and often meditate to find the answer. Even then, there might not be a fixed answer, or there might be multiple answers. And remember, what you see is to come and is not fixed. The future can still be changed, and what you see when doing divination is only what might come if the same path is followed.

It is also important to note that you might not like the answers you get. And, when you are asking questions before doing divination, the questions should lead to a clear answer and have the ability to be answered easily. For example, you might ask how to better find love in the future, but it would be useless to ask what the meaning of the universe is. Try to ask smaller questions to start and build to bigger questions.

More Ogham Letters

Before we get started with divination, we need to add some additional letters to our alphabet. As with the tree alphabet, these letters are all made up of straight lines, with lines branching off from the main trunk.

Ea - Eabhadh

Two horizontal lines crisscross the vertical line through the middle, one slanting diagonally up from left to right and the other slanting down from left to right.

Magic Focus: Working together, community, settling and recognizing differences, partnership, no judgment, fairness, wisdom.

Oi - Oir

Four lines on each side make two equilateral triangles on each side of the vertical line, centered around the middle.

Magic Focus: Growth and harvest, family, honor, asking questions, working together, connection, advising two parties, common purpose.

Ui - Uillean

A line comes out from the center of the vertical line, running to the right. It continues up, then left, then down, with the line not intersecting itself.

Magic Focus: Secrets, the hidden, deepest desires, healing, looking at our goals, making dreams a reality, staying true, love, leave behind distractions.

Io - Ifin

Two diagonal lines start below the center and run parallel to the right and upwards. Two more diagonal lines start above the center and run parallel to the right and down.

Magic Focus: Seeing the unseen, clarity, insight, guilt, unresolved conflict, finding closure, repairing relationships, making amends, bringing change, channeling energy.

Ae - Amhancholl

A grid of lines four by four in a square pattern extends from the left of the vertical line.

Magic Focus: Cleansing and purification, aid in childbirth and healing, get rid of your baggage, focus on the spiritual, reassess your plans, and rise from the ashes.

I am going to show you two ways of divination, one with cards, which is very much like a tarot reading, and the other using runes as the Norse used to do). While both rely on different media, they both use the same letters, the 20 in the previous chapter and the 5 in this, and the same processes. You will channel your insight and inner spirit into the cards to divine meaning to a question. You can also not ask a question, and the spiritual world will answer a question you did not know how to ask.

Ogham Divination with a Deck of Cards

Creating Your Deck

The first thing you need to do is to create your deck of cards. To do this, you are going to need 25 pieces of card or paper. The deck will work with any stiff card, and it's recommended that you pursue *quality* as you are going to want to use this deck over and over again; you'll need something that is going to last.

You can use high-quality card stock, and you can have them laminated afterward, although you do not have to do this. You can use any card and remake the cards as needed, but better to do it once and have the cards for a long time.

The next step is to size your cards. You can buy ready-sized cards, or you can cut the cards to size from the card stock you have (I recommend anywhere between a regular playing card size up to a tarot card size.) Choose whichever size you prefer.

Once you have your cards, and it is better to have too many in case you make a mistake with some, you can start drawing on the symbols. You should consider free-drawing them over printing them as it creates a better connection with the symbol, but this is not mandatory. Draw the 25 tree letters, one on each card. You can also draw a design on the back, but the backs should all be the same to avoid subconsciously drawing cards that you want.

When you have your 25 cards, you could make a box or container to hold them in.

Using Cards for Divination

There are two ways to use the cards. The first is to ask for general guidance, and the second is to ask for an answer to a specific question.

Both methods start the same way. No matter what you are asking, you should sit comfortably and start to shuffle the cards. As you shuffle, fall into a mediative state by being conscious and mindful of the world around you. Try to clear your mind and think of what you need to be revealed.

The first method you can use is to ask for general guidance, and this is a good practice for first thing in the morning. You are going to ask a question along the lines of: "How should I go about my day?" or "What do I need to work on today?" Continue to shuffle the cards until you feel at peace, and then stop shuffling and flip over the top card of the deck. This is the guidance for your question. Check back earlier in this chapter or the previous to see what the card means.

The second method is to ask a specific question. Fall into the same meditation as before and continue to shuffle the cards. Form a specific question in your mind, and when you are ready, you can say it out loud. This could be something like: "Will I find love this year?" or "How can I pass my upcoming test?" Deal out the first three cards after you stop shuffling.

This is where it gets a little trickier. Each card has multiple meanings, and those meanings will relate to you, so you cannot rely on someone else to interpret the meaning for you. You need to dwell on the answer and act on that answer.

For example, for the question: "Will I find love this year?" you might receive an answer that talks about luck, broken relationships, and death. When you think about this, you might conclude that you need to create a rune bracelet with the luck rune to boost your luck, you need to mend a friendship, and that might lead to an introduction to someone, and you need to renew yourself and exercise more, boosting your confidence and possibly meeting other people.

Ogham Divination with Runes

Creating Your Runes

To create your runes, you are going to use pieces of branches. In a perfect world, you would be able to find 25 different trees, matching them to the 25 different letters of the tree alphabet, but you do not need to do this. It would be very cool if you did, but it is not mandatory.

What is mandatory is collecting 25 branches, or branches that can be split into 25 pieces. Don't worry; you'll learn about a low-budget cheat at the end of this section. Now, there are a few things to think about here. You should only take from nature what it gives you, and you should not disrupt the ecosystem. This means that it is better to take branches that have already fallen or roots that have detached. The second thing to think about is the size. The pieces should be a little thicker than a pencil, but not as long. You should be able to carve runes into each of them, but they should all fit into a bag that you can carry around with you.

When you have your 25 pieces of wood (or fewer but longer pieces), you need to cut them to size. Trim them all so they are around the same length, and do not worry if they are not all exactly the same shape, although they should all be relatively straight.

Next, you should carve or draw runes on each of them, one letter for each piece. You can also decorate the sticks by adding ribbons or string to the end or painting the ends. As long as they will not get tangled up, you will be able to use them easily.

When you have your 25 runes, keep them in a bag or box so they stay together and are ready to use.

Low-budget Tip: Instead of using branches and cutting them or buying sticks, you can use popsicle sticks that you collect.

Using Runes for Divination

Now you are ready to use your sticks for divination. Just as you did with the cards, you are going to phrase a question in one of two ways. The first is to ask for general guidance, and the second is to ask a more specific question.

If you are asking for general guidance, go into the same meditative state as when dealing with a card and ask for guidance. This could be something like: "What should I foster in others?" or "What should I look out for today?" When you say your question out loud, reach into your bag or box and pull out one of the sticks. That is the answer to your question.

For the second method, there are two ways you can do this. Both require you to meditate on the question and then ask it: "How can I get a promotion at work?" or "When is it best to contact the spirits?" When you say your question out loud, reach into the bag or box and take out three sticks. You will then have to interpret them to reach your answer.

The second way to approach this question is to say your question out loud and then dump the sticks onto the ground in front of you. Look down at the sticks and find patterns in the layout of the sticks that resemble tree letters. You might find more or less than three patterns, and that is okay. Use what you find to interpret the answer to your question.

As with anything of worth, you need to practice this skill to get better at it. When you first start out, you might not understand the answers that you are given, but you will not yet understand all that is Druidry. Do not become discouraged. The more you do this, the more sense it will make. Practice divination, and it will begin to become obvious to you.

Chapter 9: Sacred Days and How to Celebrate Them Alone

Just like any religion or belief system, there are holidays and special days associated with Druidry. Just because you are a Hedge Druid does not mean that you cannot celebrate them alone. You can be a practicing Hedge Druid and have a community around you that are not Druids, and you might invite them to celebrate with you, or you might celebrate within the astral plane. And there is nothing wrong with just celebrating the holidays by yourself; some alone time can do wonders for the spirit.

The pagan calendar is represented by a wheel, The Wheel of the Year, and you can think about the wheel as being split up by eight spokes, spaced equally. At the end of each spoke is a date, and on that date falls a Druid holiday. Four of these holidays celebrate the seasons, one for each season, and the other four are historical holidays. As the seasonal holidays correspond to the seasons, you will find that they are celebrated at different times in the Northern and Southern hemispheres. You will also find pagan holidays that greatly influence the holidays in most modern religions. You can celebrate each of the eight holidays by yourself or with other people.

The Wheel of the Year includes the following important dates:

- **February 1st - 2nd:** Imbolc
- **March 19th - 23rd:** Ostara
- **April 30th – May 1st:** Beltane

- **June 19th - 23rd:** Litha/Midsummer
- **August 1st - 2nd:** Lughnasadh
- **September 20th - 24th:** Mabon
- **October 31st - November 1st:** Samhain
- **December 19th - 23rd:** Yule

One of the most important things to know as a Druid is that nothing is mandatory. If there are some holidays that you do not want to celebrate, you do not need to celebrate them. If you want to celebrate them all, then go ahead. In essence, you can tailor each holiday, and most of Hedge Druidry, to yourself.

Most Druid holidays are about celebrating what we have and being thankful for the harvest. When we look at ancient Druids, it is easy to see why food is so celebrated and why it is part of the celebration. Food was not as easy to come by hundreds of years ago, and having food was a celebration in itself. At the most basic level, you can celebrate each of the holidays by having food by yourself, sharing food, or feasting with others. Each festival is about being thankful, so you can show gratitude while you eat by thinking about what you are thankful for. That is a good habit to get into whenever you are sitting down to eat.

Imbolc

When the sun goes down on February 1st, Imbolc has begun. This is the first holiday of the year, and it is a time to start celebrating as we are halfway out of winter and halfway toward spring. Think back to the ancient Druids and how excited they must have been for the coming of spring and how they would look at all the seeds they could plant and the plants and flowers that would grow.

Imbolc is also known as the Feast of Brigid, and as the name suggests, you can host a feast on this holiday. Of course, if you are celebrating by yourself, you can have your own feast and only cook enough food for yourself to feast on. When you are feasting on Imbolc, you can also honor the goddess Brigid by offering some food and drink to her. Simply set out a plate and glass and fill both a little as a gesture to the goddess or perform one of the rites or rituals detailed in a later chapter.

There are many festivals within the Druid calendar that are considered fire festivals, and Imbolc is one of them. Traditionally, Druids and other Celtic celebrants would light a fire to stave off the cold and dark. This is why some festivals are considered fire festivals. You can play into this by hosting a bonfire (safely) if you want to have a community event, although you can have a bonfire by yourself too, or you can represent the fire by lighting a candle.

As we are celebrating midwinter, we are looking to the coming warmth and longer days. This is a good festival to be introspective and consider your growth both in the previous years and for the coming year. If you like to make plans for your growth over the year and beyond, it can be a good idea to involve that in your celebration. Have a journal ready and think about yourself and how you want to grow over the coming months. Use this thought process as a celebration. Just as our ancestors would celebrate the coming spring, we should celebrate the coming growth within ourselves.

Ostara

The dates of Ostara will change according to the hemisphere, with the celebration coming in March in the Northern Hemisphere but falling in September in the Southern Hemisphere, and some of the timing can depend on the sun. Ostara is also known as the Spring Equinox and was a very important time for our ancestors. This was the start of spring, a time when they could plant their seeds and look forward to a bountiful harvest later in the year.

You might also notice that Easter sounds a lot like Ostara, and that is not a coincidence. Much of religion has been taken from pagan traditions, and while we are not invalidating the celebration of Easter as a religious holiday, it is known that the date of the celebration was chosen to coincide with the pagan celebration to allow for more open celebrations when people of faith were persecuted.

You will also see a lot of similar symbolism during Ostara. Eggs are used in many decorations, symbolizing the new growth that comes during spring. The inception and hatching of an egg can be compared directly to sowing seeds and harvesting. If you are decorating your house, or even just your table, you can use eggs, eggshells, egg shapes, and egg drawings. You can also incorporate eggs into your meals for the day.

The celebration of Ostara is named after the Germanic goddess Ostara, the goddess of spring. She was the one who brought the spring and was worshipped as a result.

Many temples and places of worship were aligned with the sun and the equinoxes, and you might even find some structures close to you that are such, and you can search them out when you are celebrating the day. If you want to celebrate alone, you can be outside in the sun, and it is traditional to be up early enough to watch the sunrise and even stay outside until the sun sets. You can also feast on this day, though you might also choose to fast if you want to focus on the time when food might have been scarcer. Whatever you do, ensure that you spend some of the days outside.

Beltane

From the time the sun rises on April 30th until the sun sets on May 1st and on the opposite side of the calendar in the Southern Hemisphere, Beltane is in effect. The Spring Equinox is behind us, and the Summer Solstice is in front of us.

There are a few ways to celebrate Beltane. Some see it as a festival of the days getting longer – of more light and personal growth. Others connect the festival to fertility, both in ourselves and the world around us. We can choose to try and conceive during Beltane if we are having trouble with fertility, or we can recognize the fertility inside in the form of our ideas and thoughts.

Just as you journaled at Imbolc, you can also journal during Beltane. Let the festival spark your imagination, and take the time to be alone with yourself and focus on your ideas. Hone your ideas so that you can make plans for the rest of the year. Or focus on the fertility around you. You can use the celebration as a time to plant seeds both inside and outside. Start growing flowers, herbs, or plants.

Beltane is another fire festival, so you can celebrate with a bonfire or other representation of fire. At this time of the year, people were concerned with crops and animals, which were their livelihood. To ward off evil spirits from stealing crops or animals, they would light bonfires. As you light a candle or host a bonfire, spend the time thinking about how you can better protect those around you or even yourself.

You can dedicate yourself to charity around this time and try to better help the people of the world.

Litha (Midsummer)

Litha, Midsummer, and The Summer Solstice are all names for the same festival. This day will generally fall around June 21st in the Northern Hemisphere and December 21st in the Southern Hemisphere. As one of the names suggests, it is the middle of summer, and it is also the longest day of the year.

During spring, our ancestors would have been planting crops ready to be harvested in the fall. Midsummer marked the end of the planting season, and the crops would be watered from this date on. Because of this, the celebration is closely associated with water. If you have planted anything, water them on this day and other days, too, and be mindful of what you are doing. If you have planted fruits or vegetables, thank the earth and water for growing the foods that will later nourish you.

You can also center your celebrations on water. Many people make pilgrimages to sacred water sites, and if you can find one in your area, you can take the trip too. If you are a Hedge Druid who wants to celebrate alone, you can forgo the crowds and visit a body of water that you would not normally visit. You might opt to take a swim in a lake, float down a river on a boat, or spend the day at the beach. When you do, be thankful for the water for all it brings.

You should also be mindful of the coming darkness. This is nothing to fear, but the celebration of Midsummer means the days are getting shorter from here out. Stay up until the sun sets to get the most from your day, and revisit your journal that you wrote in during Imbolc to make sure that you are following through with your growth, as Litha is also a celebration of your personal growth.

Lughnasadh

Midsummer is behind us, and the Autumn Equinox approaches. This festival starts on July 31st when the sun has set and continues until the sun sets again on August 1st. While the days are getting shorter, this was a time of great celebration. The crops would be growing and almost ready to be harvested, and that would mean there would be food for the winter, ensuring survival.

Because we are looking toward the harvest, images of grains and other crops are often used around this time. You can use corn husks or cobs to decorate your house. You can fashion decorations from the husks or create writhes from wheat. While our ancestors might not have made popcorn, you can decorate with that too.

Part of the name of the holiday translates as gathering, and it is traditional during this time to be with people, so you can invite people over to eat with you, or if you do not want to celebrate with other people, you can practice your astral travel and see if there are other beings or spirits who can celebrate with you.

Even if you do not want to have people around, you can still incorporate people into your celebrations. The harvest is approaching, and that is a gift to us. You can symbolize that by giving gifts to others. You might bake up some muffins from wheat flour, or gift a loaf of bread, or a handmade decoration, perhaps. And, as you are giving, think about your own gratitude. What are you thankful for? And what has this year brought you? What are you looking forward to? You can record these thoughts in your journal.

Mabon

Mabon, or the Autumn Equinox, happens around September 22nd in the Northern Hemisphere and around March 22nd in the Southern Hemisphere. The exact dates might change from year to year. This is the time of year when the days and nights are of equal length.

The festival is also a celebration of the harvest. People would have harvested all the crops by now and stored them for the winter. Food was plentiful, and some of that food would have been put to good use as part of a feast. In the olden days, people would gather, and everyone would contribute. You can do the same by hosting a potluck where everyone brings a dish to share. If you do not want to celebrate with other people, you can cook food for others. Gift dishes to family and friends, take food around to a neighbor, or provide food to the homeless. If you have more than you need, you can celebrate this festival by being grateful for what you have and sharing it.

This is a time of transitions as we head toward winter, so check in again with your journal and ensure you are following through on what you set out to do. If you are not, look inside and try to figure out why not. If you are not, you do not need to worry about it; simply change what you are doing so that you are still growing. This is a time of transitions, after all, and you do not want to become discouraged.

Samhain

In many cultures, you will find people celebrate Halloween at this time, around October 31st in the North and May 1st in the South. Halloween is generally celebrated on the evening of the 31st, but Samhain goes longer. It starts at sundown on the 31st and continues until sundown on November 1st. The Autumn Equinox is behind us, and we are starting to look toward winter and protect ourselves against the short days and the darkness.

Of course, we do not need to protect ourselves in the same way as our ancestors did. When the winter came, it could be a tough time where people were susceptible to the cold, and threats could strike more easily in the darkness. This is a spiritual time of year, and many people feel closer to the dead during this time. Halloween and Day of the Dead are also celebrated around this time.

This is a good time to visit your ancestors. Revisit the altar you created and spend some time with those who have passed. Be sure to take some offerings to them, perhaps some bread and wine. You can also practice your astral travel during this time, and the barrier between the physical and spiritual worlds is thinner.

And the theme of death is not just focused on death; it is also about change and rejuvenation. In spring, we are growing, but in autumn, we are changing. Revisit your plans and be prepared to overhaul them. Reflect on yourself and think about what you need as a person.

Yule

You might associate Yule with Christmas, and it has become connected, but only because Christmas has borrowed so heavily from Yule. Yule is also known as the Winter Solstice and falls around December 21st and June 21st on the other side of the world.

This is the last holiday or festival of the year, and it is a time to look forward to the next year. Today is the shortest day of the year, and that means that the days are going to start getting longer, and the light is coming back to the world.

You might be familiar with a yule log, a long cake fashioned to look like a log. The inspiration for this dessert comes from a yule log, a log that was decorated and placed on your hearth. Some people would bring a whole tree into their home instead of just a log, and that is where the tradition of the Christmas tree comes from.

You can celebrate Yule by bringing a log into your home and decorating it. It is traditional to place the yule log on your hearth. If you do not have a hearth, you can place it anywhere in your home, perhaps on your table, as you prepare food for others or just for yourself. You can decorate your log with anything you like, but try to keep it natural and think about the look and smell. You can add berries to the log for some color, dried fruit for the aroma, and other herbs and spices. When Yule is over, you can burn the log for fuel if you have a fireplace or burn it outside to symbolize the end of yule.

Celebrating Eisteddfod

Eisteddfod is celebrating what it means to be a bardic Druid. This is an optional festival, so there is no need to celebrate it if you do not want to. But, if you do decide to celebrate the event, you can do so as part of a community or celebrate alone. You do not even need to celebrate it with other Druids if there are none around. As a Hedge Druid, you can still celebrate with people of all faiths and beliefs. There are no religious connotations to the festival, so everyone can join in.

Eisteddfod is basically a calibration of the bards. You might remember from some earlier writings that a bard is someone who can talk, inspire, share orally, and entertain. That might seem like a lot, and you might be picturing someone like a court jester in olden times or someone today with a lot of talent, but that has nothing to do with what it really means to be a bard. If you are orating, telling stories, reading aloud, or anything of that nature, then you are already a bard. Following the bardic life means constantly improving your skills, so if you are doing that, you are a Druid bard. And it is often when things go wrong that you become the most entertaining or have the most room to improve.

And, if you really do not want to do any of this in front of anyone else, you can sing or read or orate alone or to the spirits. Instead of reading a poem to a group of people, you can go into nature and read to the spirits. Or you might sit at your ancestral altar and read a story to those who have come before you. You could even dedicate a song or reading to the gods and goddesses.

Celebrating Eisteddfod?

Basically, this celebration is a coming together of bards to share in song, story, poem, and any other kind of performance. As a Hedge Druid, you might not have any other Druids to celebrate with, or you might not want to celebrate with any other Druids. In this case, you have two main options. You can invite non-Druids to participate with you – or you can participate alone. Both are valid and will help with your personal development.

In Wales, Eisteddfods are held around the year, and the larger ones are competitive. It is not necessary to be competitive during an Eisteddfod, and when you are starting out, you should not have any competition at the event. As you progress on your journey, you might go to an Eisteddfod competition or host your own. Of course, with anything of this nature, the best performance is usually subjective, and the point is to have fun over winning.

If you want to create some community through an Eisteddfod, a great way of doing so is around a campfire or a bonfire. The scene is already set. As the stars come out above, the flames warm people and provide some illumination, the perfect tableau for telling stories. Fire is also a place where people naturally like to gather, and it often inspires creativity in people.

At the most basic level, you can tell stories about the fire. You might have sat around a fire and had people tell stories one by one without noticing it, and this is already an Eisteddfod. But, if you are hosting one, you want to be more deliberate about it and give people time to prepare. Everyone should have a chance to perform something, as short or as long as they like. You could read a poem from a book, tell a humorous story, sing a song, dance, tell jokes, act something out, or perform in some other way. This is a chance to share, so make sure everyone is given respect as they share what they have brought.

You do not need to have the Eisteddfod around a fire; you can host anywhere you want. You can even combine the festival with one of the festivals or holidays mentioned above as a way to celebrate the holiday, and if you do, you can tailor the performances to the holiday.

If you celebrate with other people who are not Druids, you are essentially still a Hedge Druid. If you are a Hedge Druid but want to step out of that and form a Druid community, then an Eisteddfod is a great way to do so.

If you want to do this alone, that is fine too. You can still celebrate Eisteddfod as part of one of the other holidays. You can do it at home with food, or you can sit by the fire by yourself. Sometimes, solitude helps breed the most creativity. Because you are alone, you do not need to tailor your performance to the audience. You can perform any way you like, and you can use this performance as practice for Eisteddfods, where you will be performing in front of other people.

If you are still worried about getting started, you can start with a simple poem reading. Choose your favorite poem, and instead of reading it internally, read it aloud. You will likely find the process empowering.

One key thing to remember is that Eisteddfod is a celebration of being a Druid bard, so if you find that you are not enjoying the process, then the bardic life might not be for you, and there is no shame in admitting that. In fact, it shows strength to be able to leave something behind and focus on other areas of your Druid journey. If this celebration makes you a better Druid, continue, and if it does not, try something else.

Chapter 10: Spells and Rituals

Once you become a Druid, you can manipulate the world around you in many ways. Now, before we begin, it's important that you understand that you aren't going to be able to create fireballs that will slay dragons. This is magic that works with nature and is not destructive in any way. The Druid way is subtle and helpful. Everything is done with minimal disturbance.

Spells are important to perform Druid magic.
https://unsplash.com/photos/D6sF071Cmds

If you have not been put off by the lack of fireballs, read on to find out how you can perform Druid magic.

Rituals

Ritual of Soul Healing

Use this ritual to heal grief.

Have you ever felt that your soul was in need of healing? That can come after only slight injuries to your physical, mental, and emotional state. This ritual is a good way to take care of your spirit and repair it when needed. It is a good ritual to do on a regular basis just to ensure that you remain balanced.

What You Need: Rosemary, sage, thyme, twine, scissors, candles, incense

Preparation: The rosemary, sage, and thyme can be fresh or dried, but they need to be in sprigs. Bind the three of them together with the twine.

The Ritual:

1. Draw yourself a bath.
2. Surround the bath with incense and candles. This step is optional but prepare the bath so that you will be as comfortable as possible).
3. Place your herb bundle in the bath.
4. Get into the bath and lay back, and relax with your eyes closed.
5. Chant: "Rosemary, thyme, and sage, bundle up my grief and take it from me."
6. Think about your grief and acknowledge it.
7. Ask the rosemary to remind you of the person associated with the grief. You can use your own words here, and as you talk about the person or thing, feel the rosemary absorbing that and giving you images of that person or event.
8. Ask the sage to help cleanse you of the feeling of grief, and feel the sage absorbing the grief as you speak the words out loud.
9. Ask the thyme to give you the strength to carry on with your life, so you can face similar events again with wisdom and grace.
10. Relax in your bath and let whatever feelings come next wash over you.

Ritual of Balance

Use this ritual to balance yourself during the Spring Equinox.

This is a ritual that you perform at a specific time of the year, so it's recommended that you do it every year to get the most from it. You are going to perform this on the Spring Equinox when the balance between night and day is the same. This is a good way to center yourself and look to the future.

What you need: an altar (see the previous chapter on creating an altar) and offerings of bread or honey and mead or wine.

Preparation: You need to find a space where you are not going to be disturbed. This is best done outside so that you can be under the sun when doing this ritual. You are going to leave your altar where it is all day, so make sure that no one is going to stumble across it.

The Ritual:

1. Before the sun rises, go out to the space you are going to use and set up your altar and offerings. You could also do this on the previous day if you do not have the time to do it on the same day.
2. When you lay out your offering, offer it up to nature, using your own words to do so.
3. When the sun starts to rise, acknowledge it: *"I know today is a day of balance, and that starts with the coming of the light. The days will start to get longer, and that means there are infinite possibilities ahead of me."*
4. Chant *"Gywar"* (Goo-yar) over and over while thinking about the power of the sun as it hits you. Gywar translates to flow.
5. Stand in the sun for as long as you want, feeling it bathe you in its light. Be mindful. You should not stare at the sun but see what it illuminates as it rises and notices how the colors change as the sun rises in the sky.
6. If you have the time, do some meditation of your choice.
7. Come back in time for the sunset.
8. Chant *"Calas"* (Cay-lass) over and over many times ads you want. Calas translates to grounding.
9. You might want to take your shoes off at this point if you have not already. Feel the ground beneath your feet and be mindful of it. The darkness is coming, but that is only a transition, and we welcome

that.

10. Finish by packing up your altar and offerings.

Ritual of Water Healing

Use this ritual to bring healing both to yourself and the land.

When you are conversing and communing with nature, you will get a sense of how nature is reacting to the world around it. This is a good ritual to help nature maintain balance, and it can also help to heal you of any physical aches and pains you might be experiencing. You can do this around any water source, but it will be particularly powerful around the water sources you find to be sacred.

What You Need: Container for water, herbs, and plants of your choice

Preparation: It is important to spend time in nature first and to be able to commune with nature before you attempt this ritual. It is not going to go wrong, but you can waste your time if you are trying to heal what is not broken. Spend the time to find water sources that are out of balance before you decide where to heal. Also, consult our list of sacred plants and herbs, or do your own research to decide what plants and herbs would be best to use, depending on the imbalance you find. Boil up some water and add the herbs to it. Let the water cool and place it in the container to take with you.

The Ritual:

1. Find a spot along with the water source where you are not going to be disturbed.

2. It is optional to set up an altar along with the water source, but make sure you are in a place where the altar is not going to be disturbed.

3. Meditate first before you continue with this ritual. Be mindful of the water as you sit beside it. Feel the spray on your face, listen to the babbling, see the flow, and touch the water to feel its coolness. You should feel a connection to the source of water before you move on.

4. Take two rocks (or any two other objects) and knock them together in time with your heartbeat. Over time, you might notice that the heartbeat strays from yours, and you should let it. This is the heartbeat of the water.

5. Pour your water tincture into the water source.

6. As you add the water, recite any words that come to mind or you think might be appropriate for the healing.
7. Place your hand in the water and try to feel your mixture flowing away and into the water source as a whole. Close your eyes and try to see the healing in your mind. Think about the ecosystem as a whole, and as you do, feel your own body being healed too as you become one with the water.
8. Repeat the heartbeat by knocking the two stones together again. You can continue this for as long as it feels right.
9. Thank nature and thank the spirits for allowing you to be a part of the process and for giving you the skills and tools to help heal something much bigger than you.
10. Take your tools and leave the space as you found it.

Ritual of Blessing

Use this ritual to heal and bless the land around you.

You should be thankful for what nature has given you, and it should be a regular part of your Hedge Druidry practice to perform healing and blessing rituals. You will find that when you are blessing the land regularly, you will find it easier to visit with the spirits, commune with nature, and be more prepared for astral travel.

What You Need: Branches, herbs, plants, dried flowers, pine cones, all fallen in nature, natural twine or binding, a lighter, wax (optional)

Preparation: You want to create a bundle that will burn or smoke. Everything that you use in the bundle should be natural and should have fallen naturally, so do not go around and pluck twigs or herbs, but find that which nature has discarded. Take all of the natural materials you have gathered and combine them. You might be able to bind them together in sprigs, but if you have items like pine cones, you might have to bundle them into packages and add wax to hold them together. You are also going to need a fire, and you need to be outside. This is a perfect ritual to combine with one of the fire festivals described in a previous chapter, as you will already have a fire, but it can be done anytime.

The Ritual:

1. Find your spot. You want to be out in nature, but you want to be careful too. If you can find a place with a fire pit, that is great. This is a great ritual to do while you are camping.
2. Light your fire and wait until it has burned down to coals.

3. State your intentions before you add your bundle. You might want to become more attuned with the land, just want to bless it, or show your gratitude for what the land gives.
4. Add your bundle on top of the coals.
5. As the bundle burns, watch the fire and look out for shapes, symbols, or massages you are able to interpret. Nature might try to send you messages through the flames.
6. If you feel like it, you can also sing, dance, perform, drum, etc.
7. Allow the fire to burn out before you leave, and always remember to leave the space as you found it.

Spells

Protection Spell - Onion Braid

You can use this spell to protect your home on a daily basis, or you can be more intentional and craft multiple onion braids to protect you when you are traveling the astral plane. *Recommendation: placing one at each threshold of your home or placing four around you in the cardinal directions if you are traveling the astral plane.*

You need onions with the green tops still attached and a long length of twine or string. You will tie the onions one by one to the twine and string, tying at least seven onions to the string. The important thing here is to incant your intentions into the onions as you are tying them.

If you want to protect your home, use your words to bind the intention into the onions. If it is specifically to protect you while you are traveling, incant that. You can also braid onions if you want to protect a person, but it might not be practical for them or you to wear a string of onions around your neck.

Protection Oil

This is a great tincture for when you are traveling in the spiritual realm or when you feel under attack from spiritual energy. You can wear it in a vial around your neck, dab it on your skin, or spray it around your home. Not only will it add protection, but it smells really good too.

You Will Need: ¼ cup of carrier oil of your choice (like jojoba), three drops patchouli, three drops lavender, two drops mugwort, and one drop lemon oil.

Blend the oils together, and as you do, think about why you need protection. Be mindful when you are mixing the oil, and try to allow that thought to flow into the oil and bind itself there. Once the oil is mixed, you can store it in a vial or a spray bottle if you are using it around your home – and store it in a dark and cool place.

Musical Spell - Happiness

If you feel unhappy in your life or you want to inspire happiness in others, you can incorporate music into the proceedings. This is a great spell if you feel you are a bardic Druid, though you do not need to be adept at music to cast this spell. It relies on the beating of a drum, and you can use a drum or anything else to create a drum beat. And do not worry if you are not musical at all; you only need to focus on the intention of the spell.

What You Need: Incense, a lighter, ribbons, a drum, or something to substitute as a drum.

Light the incense. You can choose any incense you like for this spell, but you should try and match it to the person who is to benefit from the spell. Either go with what you like for the spell or ask the person what they would like.

Tie colorful ribbons to the drum or the items you are substituting for the drum. This might not appear to make a difference to the spell, but the addition of bright colors injects some fun and helps you to focus your intentions.

Start playing the drum. You do not have to be the best drummer, but if you cannot find a good rhythm, try to feel your heartbeat and beat the drum along to that. If you do not need something to help your rhythm, you can just start with a slow beat that might mimic a heartbeat.

Feel the drum vibrate, and allow those vibrations to rise up through your body. If the spell is for you, feel the vibrations breaking through the sadness within you. If it is for someone else, try to exude the vibrations, and this is where the intentions matter more than the musical talent. The great thing about this spell is that you can do it at a distance. You are sending the vibrations and intent out into the world.

Close your eyes and try to feel the beating. If you need to go faster or slower, listen to your intuition and go with it. Sometimes, you might feel the nature spirits of fae-folk singing or dancing along with you. The more you convene with them, the more they will be likely to join.

Do Your Research

I have only touched on a few spells and rituals here. There are hundreds of them out there for you to discover, but that is beyond the scope of this book. Start with the basics of Druidry before you start with the more difficult and powerful spells. The more you practice the basics, the more you are going to be able to master the harder stuff.

And, with most things, the spells and rituals are not going to come to you immediately. They might, but it is unlikely. So, do not lose heart if something does not work the first time. You need to practice everything in life, and Druidry is a journey. In fact, we could call it a practice as you are going to be practicing it for your entire life. There is no one out there who has mastered the art of Druidry.

Conclusion

So, we reach the end of the book; it's been good to have had you along for the journey, and I hope that you will pick this book up again and again throughout your journey and refer to it as you grow as a Hedge Druid. Just by getting this far, you have taken massive steps on your path to Hedge Druidry. The only thing to do now is to put what you have learned into practice.

You now know a little about what it means to be a Druid and where Druidry came from. This is going to help you better understand the evolution of a Druid from ancient times to the modern-day and also connect you better to your ancestors of tradition. You have seen that being a Druid today is not all that different from how it used to be, and all the ways that other religions and ways of life have borrowed from the pagan life.

Druidry, in many ways, is about living a good life and tending to nature, but it does go beyond that, quite literally. Even a Hedge Druid can have some community, and it is important for you to consider the world and the people in it, but you now know that there is more than just what the eye can see. Taking your Druid journey means more than just reading and doing, you will be taking a spiritual journey too, and that means developing what is inside and physical or metaphysical journeys into the worlds that lie alongside our own.

There is a lot to take in in this book, so go back and read it again and again so that you absorb all there is; there are some important points, and not everything is going to come to you immediately.

I will be sending out happiness spells every day in the hope that one reaches you and inspires you on your journey.

Good luck!

Here's another book by Mari Silva that you might like

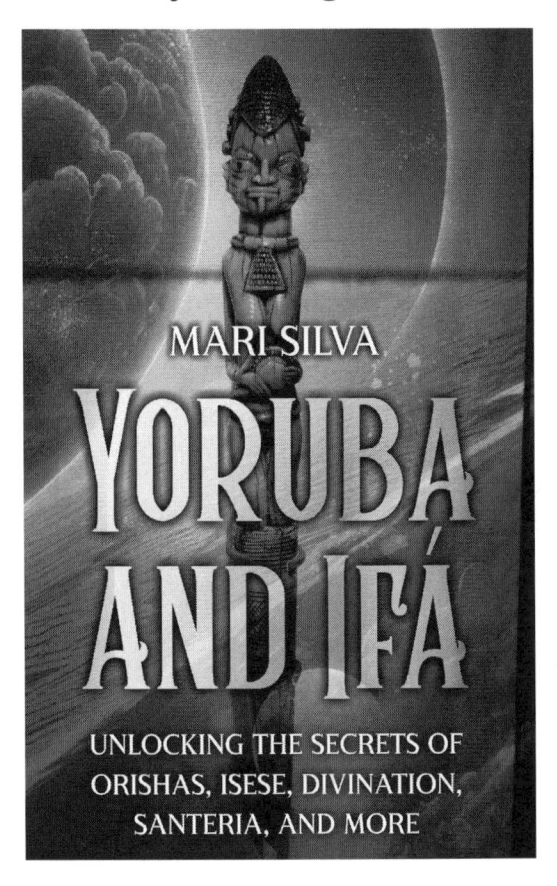

Your Free Gift
(only available for a limited time)

Thanks for getting this book! If you want to learn more about various spirituality topics, then join Mari Silva's community and get a free guided meditation MP3 for awakening your third eye. This guided meditation mp3 is designed to open and strengthen ones third eye so you can experience a higher state of consciousness. Simply visit the link below the image to get started.

https://spiritualityspot.com/meditation

References

Beth, R. (2018). The Green Hedge Witch. The Cordwood Press.

Beth, R. (2018). The Hedge Witch's Way: Magical Spirituality for the Lone Spell caster. The Cordwood Press.

Beth, R. (2018). Spell craft for Hedge Witches: A Guide to Healing Our Lives. The Cordwood Press.

De Varies, E. (2008). Hedge-Rider: Witches and the Underworld. Padraig Publishing.

Dugan, E. (2012). Garden Witch's Herbal: Green Magic, Herbalism & Spirituality. Llewellyn Worldwide.

Greenfield, T. (2014). Witchcraft Today-60 Years On. John Hunt Publishing.

Griffith, D. B. (2009). Lithe 2005. Lulu. Com.

Kane, A. (2021). Herbal Magic: A Handbook of Natural Spells, Charms, and Potions. Wellfleet Press.

Moura, A. (2014). Green Witchcraft: Folk Magic, Fairy Lore & Herb Craft. Llewellyn Worldwide.

Moura, A. (2020). Green Witchcraft IV: Walking the Faerie Path. Llewellyn Worldwide.

Moura, A. (2003). Grimoire for the Green Witch: A Complete Book of Shadows (Vol. 5). Llewellyn Worldwide.

Murphy-Hiscock, A. (2006). The Way Of The Green Witch: Rituals, Spells, And Practices to Bring You Back to Nature. Simon and Schuster.

Murphy-Hiscock, A. (2017). The green witch: your complete guide to the natural magic of herbs, flowers, essential oils, and more. Simon and Schuster

"What is Druidry?" Druidry.org, https://Druidry.org/Druid-way/what-Druidry

"About Druidry" The Druid Network, https://Druidnetwork.org/what-is-Druidry/

"Why do we know so little about the Druids?" National Geographic, https://www.nationalgeographic.com/history/article/why-know-little-Druids#:~:text=The%20word%20comes%20from%20a,from%20outsiders%2C%20particularly%20the%20Romans

"Who were the Druids?" Historic UK, https://www.historic-uk.com/HistoryUK/HistoryofWales/Druids/

"An Introduction to the Basics of Modern Druid Practice" The Druid Network, https://Druidnetwork.org/what-is-Druidry/learning-resources/shaping-the-wheel/introduction-basics-modern-Druid-practice/

"What is Awen?" The Druids Garden, https://theDruidsgarden.com/tag/what-is-awen/

"Awen" Druidry.org, https://Druidry.org/resources/awen

"The Quest for Awen." The British Druid Order, https://www.Druidry.co.uk/awen-the-holy-spirit-of-Druidry/

"A Druid's Guide to Connecting With Nature." The Druid's Garden, https://theDruidsgarden.com/2018/07/08/a-Druids-guide-to-connecting-with-nature-part-i-a-framework/

"Walking Meditation: Druidic Being in the World." Ancient Order Of Druids In America, https://aoda.org/publications/articles-on-Druidry/walking-meditation-Druidic-being-in-the-world/

"A Druid's Meditation Primer" The Druid's Garden, https://theDruidsgarden.com/2018/02/11/a-Druids-meditation-primer/

"Lesson Four ~ The Ancestors And The Living Land." The Druid Network, https://Druidnetwork.org/what-is-Druidry/learning-resources/polytheist/lesson-four/

"Ancestral Wisdom In Contemporary Druidry." Ancient Order Of Druids In America, https://aoda.org/publications/articles-on-Druidry/ancestral-wisdom-in-contemporary-Druidry/

"The Intention Of Druid Rites" Grove Of Nova Scotia Druids

"How To Find My Your Spirit Animal" What Is My Spirit Animal, https://whatismyspiritanimal.com/how-to-find-your-spirit-animal-complete-guide/

"Astral Projection Basics." Celtic Connection, https://wicca.com/meditation/astral.html

"Grounding Exercises." Living Well, https://livingwell.org.au/well-being/mental-health/grounding-exercises/

"Pagan Holidays and Thee Wheel of the Year For Beginners." The Peculiar Brunette, https://www.thepeculiarbrunette.com/pagan-holidays-and-the-wheel-of-the-year/

"About Us." Eisteddfod, https://eisteddfod.wales/about-us

"The Gaelic Tree Alphabet." Darach Social Croft, https://darachcroft.com/news/the-gaelic-tree-alphabet

"Plant Lore." The Druid Way, https://Druidry.org/Druid-way/teaching-and-practice/Druid-plant-lore

"The Use of Herbs." The Druid Network, https://Druidnetwork.org/what-is-Druidry/learning-resources/polytheist/lesson-fourteen

Made in the USA
Middletown, DE
11 September 2024